Rethinking Public Private Partnerships

RETHINKING ECONOMICS

This series is a forum for innovative scholarly writing from across all substantive fields of economics. The series aims to enrich the study of the discipline by promoting a cutting-edge approach to economic thought and analysis. Academic scrutiny and challenge is an essential component in the development of economics as a field of study, and the act of re-thinking and re-examining principles and precepts that may have been long-held is imperative.

Rethinking Economics showcases authored books that address the field from a new angle, expose the weaknesses of existing concepts and arguments, or 'reframe' the topic in some way. This might be through the introduction of radical ideas, through the integration of perspectives from other fields or even disciplines, through challenging existing paradigms, or simply through a level of analysis that elevates or sharpens our understanding of a subject.

Titles in the series include:

Rethinking Wealth and Taxes
Inequality, Globalization and Capital Income
Geoffrey Poitras

Rethinking Public Private Partnerships
Mervyn K. Lewis

Rethinking Public Private Partnerships

Mervyn K. Lewis

Emeritus Professor, University of South Australia and Emeritus Fellow, Academy of the Social Sciences in Australia

RETHINKING ECONOMICS

Edward Elgar
PUBLISHING

Cheltenham, UK • Northampton, MA, USA

Published by
Edward Elgar Publishing Limited
The Lypiatts
15 Lansdown Road
Cheltenham
Glos GL50 2JA
UK

Edward Elgar Publishing, Inc.
William Pratt House
9 Dewey Court
Northampton
Massachusetts 01060
USA

A catalogue record for this book
is available from the British Library

Library of Congress Control Number: 2021938830

This book is available electronically in the **Elgar**online
Economics subject collection
http://dx.doi.org/10.4337/9781789906400

ISBN 978 1 78990 639 4 (cased)
ISBN 978 1 78990 640 0 (eBook)

Printed and bound by CPI Group (UK) Ltd, Croydon, CR0 4YY

Contents

Figures

Tables

Boxes

Preface

When in 2019 I finished the volume *Religion and Finance: Comparing the Approaches of Judaism, Christianity and Islam*, co-authored with Ahmad Kaleem (Edward Elgar Publishing), I thought that would be my last book. Perhaps I should have stuck with that resolution. However, Edward Elgar invited me to contribute to the Rethinking series by writing a volume on *Rethinking Public Private Partnerships*. I was initially reluctant, but after looking at some recent work on PPPs, and being generally unimpressed, I changed my mind.

I should quickly add that the writings of Graeme Hodge and Carston Greve on PPPs do not fall into this category of disappointing me. While not citing chapter and verse in this book, reading their works has been instructive and their careful scholarship speedily helped me to get up to date with recent literature. The same is true of the volumes by Levitt, Scott and Garvin (2019) and also Clark and Hakim (2019), in which Tristan Gleeson, Darrin Grimsey and I contributed a chapter.

Two people in particular deserve mention. Darrin Grimsey is the first. He introduced me to PPPs and taught me most of what I know on the topic. He has also given me a practitioner's perspective on this vexed topic which, as an academic, I could not otherwise have gained.

Then, of course, I must once again give special thanks to my wife, Kay, who has, as always, been a faithful scribe and kept the large number of references under control.

Glossary

Alliance contract: Alliancing is a 'relationship contract' that effectively becomes a joint venture operating under a cost-plus, no-blame, no-dispute and good-faith basis.

Asset recycling: Governments themselves build the infrastructure and, after it is tried and tested, sell it to investors wanting to buy 'mature' infrastructure assets.

Behavioural economics: Drawing on experimental evidence compiled by cognitive psychologists, behavioural economics examines the biases that arise when people form beliefs and make decisions based on those beliefs, that is, behavioural decision theory.

Benchmarking: A process of comparing a project with similar precedent projects in order to identify issues that may impact on the project.

Build, own, operate, transfer (BOOT): An arrangement whereby a facility is designed, financed, operated and maintained by a concession company. Ownership rests with the concessionaire until the end of the concession period, at which point ownership and operating rights are transferred to the government (normally without charge).

Bundling: This refers to the integration in a PPP of functions such as design, construction, financing, operations and maintenance of the facility, often in the form of a special purpose vehicle (SPV).

Business case: The business case provides an overview of a procurement approach, a preliminary view on how the project will be delivered, an analysis of the various impacts of the project, and an indication of the likely level of market interest, before significant resources are spent on its development.

Concession: Concession-based approaches are the oldest form of PPP, and a variety of arrangements are based on the concept of a fixed-term concession, using various combinations of private sector resources to design, construct, finance, renovate, operate and maintain facilities. Ownership of the facility may remain with government or be transferred to the government upon completion of the construction or at the end of the concession period.

Confirmation bias: Selective thinking where individuals or groups search out information that confirms their beliefs, and ignore or downplay information that contradicts their beliefs.

Contracting out: An 'outsourcing' arrangement in which a public agency contracts with an external supplier for the provision of goods and/or services.

Conventional procurement: A conventional (traditional) public procurement contract is one in which a public agency secures the finance directly and pays the contractor as works progress.

Civil Society Organization (CSO): A network of 47 European non-government organizations (NGOs) in 20 countries has created the European Network on Debt and Development (Eurodad).

Design, build, finance, operate, maintain (DBFOM): A form of PPP contract developed under the Private Finance Initiative (PFI) and elsewhere whereby the service provider is responsible for the design, construction, financing, operation and maintenance of an asset.

Design, build, operate, maintain (DBOM): A form of PPP in which the public sector provides finance for a capital investment project but the providers of the projects retain the design and construction, and deliver operational and maintenance elements.

European PPP Expertise Centre (EPEC): An initiative of the European Investment Bank (EIB) to stimulate discussions on PPPs, as well as foster the diffusion of best practices in this area.

Funding: The revenue sources (e.g. taxes, service charges, user payments) tapped, for example by government, to repay the finance raised to pay for the cost of building infrastructure.

Key performance indicators (KPIs): Measures developed under a performance management regime to indicate how well specified performance targets are being realized.

Long-Term Infrastructure Contract (LTIC): A PPP that bundles design, construction, financing, operations and maintenance arrangements. Same as DBFOM.

Megaproject: A large-scale complex investment project that typically costs US$1 billion or more.

National Audit Office (NAO): The UK's National Audit Office scrutinizes public spending on behalf of Parliament. Totally independent, it audits the accounts of all government departments and agencies as well as a wide range of other public bodies, and reports to Parliament on the economy, efficiency and effectiveness with which government bodies have used public money.

National Health Service (NHS): The UK's National Health Service.

Net present value (NPV): The discounted value of a stream of either future costs or future benefits, with NPV used to describe the difference between the present value of a stream of costs and the present value of a stream of benefits.

Optimism bias: The demonstrated systematic tendency for appraisers to be overoptimistic about key project parameters, including capital costs, operating costs, works duration and benefits delivery.

Output specification: The output specification sets out the range of services that government is seeking to procure and the performance levels required for each of those services.

Private Finance Initiative (PFI): A UK programme that encompassed arrangements whereby a consortium of private sector partners came together to provide an asset-based public service under contract to a public body.

Private party: The private sector entity with which the government contracts in a PPP. Traditionally the private party has been a special purpose vehicle (SPV) created specifically for the purposes of the project.

Procurement: The component of the commissioning process that deals specifically with purchasing a service from a provider. This occurs once decisions have been taken over what outcomes or outputs are to be secured and involves the negotiation of contracts.

Project finance: A way of financing capital projects that depends for its security on the expected cash flow of the project itself rather than guarantees from the borrower or third parties.

Public private partnership (PPP): A risk-sharing relationship based upon a shared aspiration between the public sector and one or more partners from the private and/or voluntary sectors to deliver a publicly agreed outcome and/or public service.

Public sector: Refers to public agencies and enterprises that are state financed, owned and controlled.

Public Sector Comparator (PSC): A hypothetical constructed benchmark to assess the value for money (VfM) of conventionally financed procurement in comparison with a privately financed scheme for delivering a publicly funded service.

Rebel: A consultancy company with expertise in PPPs and value for money (VfM) assessment. Its March 2015 report was part of EPEC's work on PPP Investment Planning, Programming, Project Selection and Preparation.

Risk: A situation involves risk if the randomness facing an economic entity can be expressed in terms of specific numerical probabilities (objective or subjective).

Risk allocation: The allocation of responsibility for dealing with the consequences of each risk to one of the parties to the contract, or agreeing to deal with the risk through a specified mechanism which may involve sharing the risk.

Special purpose vehicle (SPV): An organization that can be established as a distinct legal entity to bring together the companies involved in a PPP in order to manage the project and share the risks and rewards.

Uncertainty: There is uncertainty where an economic entity cannot assign actual probabilities to the alternative possible occurrences.

Value for money (VfM): The optimum combination of whole-life costs, risks, completion time and quality in order to meet public requirements.

Whole-of-life cycle: Costs associated with the ongoing repair and maintenance of a facility for the term of a facility's economic life.

1. Setting the scene

BACK TO BASICS

Without wishing at the outset to trivialize the discussion about public private partnerships (PPPs), there are some similarities between the issues in public infrastructure procurement and the decision of whether to employ a builder for home construction or subcontract oneself the functions of bricklaying, carpentry, roof construction, plumbing, electrical wiring and so on. Anyone who has tried to do their own subcontracting would likely agree that it is a difficult route, whereas in most forms of building and construction, there are a host of informal links that bind the subcontractors and the project managers together, including favours to be returned, and these enable the job to get done.

To illustrate, suppose that a couple purchases a block of land and wish to build a new house, or substantially renovate one, upon it. Two options present themselves. One route would be to employ a builder to do so, in which case the building firm would provide a number of services including:

- detailed design, either using an in-house designer or, less commonly these days, working in conjunction with an architect of the couple's choice;
- submitting plans to the local authority and obtaining the necessary work permits;
- site preparation, earthworks and laying down the footings;
- selecting and organizing the various trades, drawing on the firm's knowledge of the trade skills and an established relationship;
- advising on the appropriate materials and sourcing them from the best suppliers;
- sequencing the various trades;
- replacing any subcontractors unable to complete the work in a timely fashion,
- assisting with access to finance;
- undertaking maintenance should faults emerge.

Of course, the builder will not provide these services free of charge, purchasing materials at 'trade', not retail, and adding margins on to the subcontractors' costs. There is no 'free lunch'.

A seemingly cheaper option would see our couple themselves acting as project managers, seeking out and employing the trades, while perhaps leaving some of the jobs such as painting and decorating for themselves. Features of this approach are:

- cost saving from the absence of the organizing fee charged by the builder;
- increased flexibility, by being able to alter specifications without the need to renegotiate the contract with the contractor.

However, cost savings and flexibility depend on how well the couple handle the subcontracting. In particular:

- How well do our couple know the skills and capabilities of the trades?
- How difficult is it to coordinate and schedule the various trades?

Most certainly, some are tempted to go down this route, but it invariably proves to be time-consuming and not easy to pull off successfully within reasonable time constraints.

In short, the 'bundled' approach of the builder may offer greater certainty of on-time, on-cost delivery of the house, to an acceptable standard, albeit at a cost for the risk insurance supplied. Unbundling into a series of separate contracts may be cheaper, but this can put the procurer at the mercy of the subcontractors' timelines and quality standards, as well as testing the procuring couple's knowledge of the industry and the way it operates.

If confined to these two choices, I would expect that many people (and most of the risk-averse ones) would opt for the bundled services of the bespoke builder. However, an even more bundled approach may have greater appeal. This is a situation where a development company acquires a large parcel of land and subdivides it into small (and increasingly very small) blocks, including a communal reserve and recreational area. It then puts in the roads and connections to water, sewerage, power and communication facilities. A few display homes are erected and customers can select one of these, or one from a number of other designs available, which can be built on the particular site chosen by the client. Like a suit or outfit purchased 'off the peg', the design can be constructed at a relatively low cost. Our couple can then buy a complete package, sometimes with rudimentary landscaping included.

Having such a complete package on offer may be commonplace in residential construction but is rare in terms of public infrastructure, the procurement of which would normally be initiated by the public entity via a one-off transaction. Yet it is not unknown for public–private interactions to arise in other ways. In the United States, most notably, private prisons operate in a majority of states. As of 2001, there were 151 private correctional facilities with the capacity to house 119 023 prisoners or detainees. By 2017, the number of people housed in private prisons had increased to 212 718, across 28 states and the federal government, and this number represented 8.2 per cent of the total state and federal prison population (The Sentencing Project, 2019). Some of the private prisons have emerged as a result of contracts with the state in which they are located. More usually, a private corporation builds a facility in a particular state and then negotiates contracts either with that state or with another state, county or federal body to house or reserve places for prisoners from that jurisdiction, with payment on a per diem basis.

In the case of residential construction, our couple seem most likely to opt for a bundled approach in one form or another. However, this has not been the case for public infrastructure. Traditionally it has relied, at least to a large degree, on being procured using separate contracts for the different stages involved, and this approach is still the predominant mode. Now, with the advent of PPPs, an alternative has presented itself.

In later chapters I will examine how and why this different contracting arrangement came into being. But the distinction is apparent, especially in what Broadbent and Laughlin (2003, p. 340) call the Long-Term Infrastructure Contract (LTIC) type PPP.[1] Rather than there being separate design, construction, financing, operations and maintenance arrangements as occurs with traditional public procurement, these functions are combined under one contractor. This integration ('bundling') within a long-term partnership framework provides a financial motivation for the project company to think beyond the design stage and build in energy-reducing and waste-minimizing features that may cost more initially but result later in lower operating and running costs, and so deliver 'whole-of-life' cost-effectiveness over time.

On this basis, bundling can be seen as the defining characteristic of a PPP. Under the terms of a PPP contract, the private sector partner is paid for the delivery of the services to specified levels and time frame and must itself organize all the managerial, financial and technical resources needed to achieve the required standards. Importantly, the private sector bears the risks of meeting the service specification as it would for any commercial risk it undertakes and, barring exceptional circumstances (e.g. discovery of pre-existing latent defect and contamination), cannot draw upon government resources to recoup its losses.

Yet, not all bundling is the same, nor are the risks the same, despite some similarities. The most obvious difference between residential and commercial is the length of the arrangement, being 20 years or so for public infrastructure, although construction of some houses may stretch over several years, especially if there is extensive site preparation and delays due to bad weather. Houses may run into millions or tens of millions of dollars, but not hundreds of millions or billions. Also, post-construction maintenance is less with home building, if not entirely absent.

Nevertheless, notwithstanding these differences between the two types of construction, there are going to be similar attractions to the public procurer of infrastructure of going down the PPP approach and having, say, design, building, finance, operations and maintenance services combined into one contract instead of writing separate contracts for the several elements, and the more so when the bundled PPP arrangement offers 'insurance' against time and cost overruns that have been known to plague conventional procurement. It is also the case that theoretical arguments can be invoked to support this choice.

Such attractions (integrated contracting, whole-of-life costing, incentives to on-time, on-budget delivery) were the promise when LTIC-type PPPs entered the scene in the early 1990s. Opposition (indeed sometimes extreme hostility) to PPPs today may indicate that this promise was not achieved in sufficient instances. There are enough possible reasons in terms of the complexity of the contracting arrangements, inflexibility, public versus private financing costs, incomplete risk transfer, potential for opportunism (on both sides), and the time and costs of procurement, to take this suggestion seriously and accord it the attention that it warrants.

Interestingly, in some quarters PPPs were judged guilty, unfit for purpose, and condemned virtually at conception.[2] Admittedly, there are some counter-intuitive elements in the PPP. Why, in the face of evolving technology and changing requirements, would a government body make itself hostage to the future by entering into a design, build, finance, operate, maintain (DBFOM) transaction and tie its hands in this way for 20–30 years, rather than opt for the flexibility of separate contracts? For some critics, to pre-judge the answer in advance of the evidence points to the presence of ideological/political positions, perhaps encouraged by the association of PPPs with privatization. One of the earliest volumes on PPPs was entitled *Privatization and Public–Private Partnerships* (Savas, 2000). Undoubtedly, a cleavage has emerged between practitioners and academics, and within academia between the engineering literature and that of public policy writers, that needs to be recognized.

For this volume, the challenge is to see if this breach can be bridged. Probably not is the answer, but it may be possible to elucidate and treat the different viewpoints with due respect and refocus the discussion. That, at least is the aim.

A GATHERING OF CRITICS

There have always been critics of PPPs. However, it would seem that the intensity of the criticisms has grown in recent years. This is in part because of the shift in the literature from economics, engineering and construction to public policy and healthcare. PPPs were conceived as an incentive-compatible alternative to traditional procurement which had immediate appeal to economists but perhaps less so to public policy scholars and sociologists.

The intensified dislike of PPPs can partly be laid at the feet of the PPPs themselves (or maybe more correctly, those who administered them badly). As their usage increased, more problems emerged which became grist to the mill for those who opposed their introduction in the first place. Influential groupings of opponents of PPPs formed a strong, well-funded lobby group. One such European body is considered below.

The remainder of this introductory chapter looks at two reports that, to put it mildly, call PPPs to account, along with one government policy reversal, and it is fair to say that, in combination, they have served to prompt me to agree to the writing of this volume. Of the three, it is the last that is likely to have the most far-reaching consequences, both in the country itself and in other domains in which PPPs are active, and it is that with which I begin.

UK Treasury

The UK Treasury, which in 1992, under the Private Finance Initiative (PFI), effectively pioneered the use of PPPs in the modern era, announced in October 2018 that PPPs would be abolished in the sense that existing contracts for PFI and PF2 (the latest incarnations) would be honoured, but no new ones will be signed. Although portrayed by the Chancellor Philip Hammond as 'putting another legacy of Labour behind us', the reality is that it was under the Conservative government of John Major that PPPs were introduced, albeit later to be expanded under the Labour government of Tony Blair. From 61 new contracts approved in 2010 with a total value of nearly £7 billion, the latest decision signified a significant fall from grace for the PPP model, likely to resonate in other countries that followed the UK lead.

In his press release, the Chancellor made the following points about PPPs (The Guardian, 2018b). They were accused of:

- failing to deliver value for money;
- being inflexible and overly complex;
- being a source of significant fiscal risk to government;
- pushing up official government debt;
- failing to prove that private funding provided better value for money than public funding.

Earlier, oral evidence was given by senior officials to the House of Commons Public Accounts Committee (PAC), which was investigating whether PFI delivers value for money. The inquiry came amid deepening public criticism of PFI, which had been blamed for handing huge profits to private sector owners of the PFI deals and diverting funds from cash-starved public services. The committee called upon senior figures in the Treasury and the Infrastructure and Projects Authority (IPA) to give evidence, including Charles Roxburgh, the second permanent secretary at the Treasury, and Tony Meggs, the IPA's chief executive. Roxburgh said, 'We have not done a new PF2 project since April 2016, which was the last of the schools programmes. We think there are some promising projects on the horizon – some good road projects – but we are talking of a handful, rather than going back to the days of the 2000s, when it was up to one a week and £8bn a year.' Witnesses said PFI fell into disuse because it got difficult to prove that private funding provided better value for money than public funding (The Guardian, 2018a).

The CSO Report

Turning now to the two reports, the first is by the European Network on Debt and Development (Eurodad), a network of 47 European non-governmental organizations (NGOs) in 20 countries which works as part of a global move-ment to push governments and powerful institutions to adopt transformative changes to the global economic and financial system. Eurodad members are diverse, with differing sizes and constituencies and working in different political contexts, but united together behind a common mission and goals, in particular that policymakers cannot continue to ignore the social and political costs of their economic choices. The report was produced by civil society organizations (CSOs) in countries around the world, and it does not leave readers of the report in suspense as to its conclusions, carrying the title *History RePPPeated – How Public Private Partnerships Are Failing*.

Table 1.1 provides a listing and a summary of the ten case studies outlined in the report. The countries included are Columbia, France, India (2), Indonesia, Lesotho, Liberia, Peru, Spain and Sweden, and the sectors covered are edu-cation, energy, healthcare, transport, and water and sanitation. According to Eurodad (2018), 'these 10 cases illustrate the most common problems encoun-tered by PPPs. Therefore, they challenge the capacity of PPPs to deliver results in the public interest' (p. 2).

Backing up the report are 239 detailed notes and references to articles and other research materials. In view of the herculean task (for one person) of tracking down and checking out all these materials, it would be churlish not to accept the veracity of the reports, albeit with one exception. This qualification relates to the Swedish case, for which it is recorded:

In Sweden, the total construction cost of Nya Karolinska Solna (NKS) hospital has rocketed – from €1.4 billion to €2.4 billion – and has been beset by technical failures. It is now known as 'the most expensive hospital in the world'. (Ibid. p. 2)

Table 1.1   *Ten Eurodad case studies summarized*

Project	Critique by civil society organizations
1. Liberia Education Advancement Programme (Liberia)	PPP involved outsourcing Liberian public pre-primary (kindergarten) and primary schools for a one-year pilot programme run by a for-profit American-based company. While there was an improvement in teaching and learning outcomes, higher salaries paid ended up too expensive for government to maintain.
2. Tata Mundra Ultra Mega Power Project (India)	Five coal-based thermal power stations were built and operated. Social and marine impact assessments ignored risk to marine environment and destruction of mangroves, impacting fishing communities and drinking water. Increases in the prices of imported coal caused financial losses and higher electricity prices to government procurers and ultimately consumers. Risk allocation questionable.
3. The Offshore Gas Storage Castor Project (Spain)	Feted as Spain's largest offshore gas storage plant, gas injections during start-up operations resulted in more than 1000 earthquakes in an area on the coast of the Valencian community and Catalunya, and suspension of the gas injections. The operator renounced the contract and sought compensation that was paid 'unjustly' when the facility was taken into public ownership and never used.
4. Nya Karolinska Soina (NKS) Hospital (Sweden)	Decision to use PPP was guided by belief that the model would give three benefits: certainty of costs, certainty to deliver and better value. However, it was over budget, over time and fees paid for the advice of consultants added to costs. Also, see text below (pp. 102–3).
5. Queen Mamohato Memorial Hospital (Lesotho)	The Queen Mamohato Hospital in Lesotho had significant adverse and unpredictable financial consequences on public funds. In 2016 the private partner Tsepong's 'invoiced' fees amount to two times the 'affordability threshold' set by the government and the World Bank at the outset of the PPP. Contributing factors to cost escalation included flawed indexation of the annual fee paid by the government to Tsepong (unitary fee) and poor forecasting.
6. The New Paris Courthouse (France)	PPP has been criticized for being too expensive, too complex and lacking transparency. Borrowing costs at 6% p.a. were much more expensive than public procurement costs of 1% p.a. The cost of outsourcing of maintenance was also higher than public provision. The construction of the courthouse proved so complex, costly and controversial that the new French Justice Minister has decided that her Ministry will never engage in a PPP again.
7. International Airport of Chinchero – Cuzco (Peru)	When the private entity failed to get adequate funds, the renegotiation process to build a new airport through a PPP in Chinchero resulted in a change to the entire funding structure of the project with the state becoming the main financing partner. After a strong report from the Comptroller General referring to economic damages for the state, and in the midst of a national scandal over the project, the Peruvian government finally had to cancel the contract on the grounds of national interest.

Project	Critique by civil society organizations
8. Navigability of the Magdalena River (Colombia)	The PPP project designed to improve the navigability of the Magdalena River (Columbia's main river) was said to have suffered from poor planning. While the project never went into the construction phase – it collapsed due to the failure of the company to get the financing needed to implement it – the preliminary dredging works carried out negatively affected the fishing environment in and around the river.
9. Jakarta's Water Supply (Indonesia)	Leading international water companies, Thames Water and Suez, signed a PPP contract in 1997 to deliver Jakarta's water supply. Promises that 70% of Jakarta's population would have piped water by 2002 were never realized, and most of the population still has no access to clean piped water and the public water utility RAM Jaya has suffered huge financial losses, some of its own making during the Asian financial crisis. Meanwhile, the original private sector companies have reaped financial rewards, with both original companies having sold either all or part of their stakes in the project.
10. Khandwa Water Supply Augmentation Project (India)	In the small Indian town of Khadwa, a PPP was launched to provide municipal water, but there was no consultation. Progress was slow and it took four years to finally inform the population about what was happening and the likely higher cost of water rates. More than 10 000 households filed objections against the project within a period of 30 days. This was in a town where regular domestic water connections totalled 15 000.

Source: Based on Eurodad (2018).

Admittedly, costs rose sharply during the construction of NKS. Yet, in a comparison of eleven new PPP hospitals built and completed between 2006 and 2018 in terms of capital expenditures per hospital bed, there were six hospitals dearer than NKS (Grimsey and Lewis, 2017). The PPP healthcare megaprojects were in London, Turkey (2), Canada (4), Sweden (1) and Australia (3). In fact, of these, the 'prize' for 'most expensive hospital in the world' belongs to my home state of South Australia in the form of the Royal Adelaide hospital (RAH), similarly a PPP. Like NKS this hospital also has 800 beds and single rooms with full facilities along with a bed for relatives to spend the night. The simple reality is that hospitals are expensive to construct, fit out and run. Hopefully, given our reliance on their reporting, the Swedish overstatement is an exception and the other information contained in the Eurodad report is accurate.

Overall, the conclusions of the CSO report are as below. These are made in the form of recommendations to the World Bank, the International Monetary Fund (IMF) and other public development banks and organizations.

• Halt the aggressive promotion and incentivizing of PPPs for social and economic infrastructure financing, and publicly recognize the financial and other significant risks that PPPs entail.

- Support countries in finding the best financing method for public services in social and economic infrastructure, which are responsible, transparent, environmentally and fiscally sustainable and in line with their human rights obligations.
- Ensure good and democratic governance is in place before pursuing large-scale infrastructure or service developments. This should be done through informed consultation and broad civil society participation and monitoring, including by local communities, trade unions and other stakeholders.
- Ensure that rigorous transparency standards apply, particularly with regard to accounting for public funds – the contract value of the PPP and its long-term fiscal implications must be included in national accounts. Contracts and performance reports of social and economic infrastructure projects should be proactively disclosed.

Ending the Executive Summary of the CSO report there is a plea:

> Finally, we urge all those concerned with justice, equality, sustainability and human rights to resist the encroachment of PPPs and to push instead for high-quality, publicly-funded, democratically-controlled, accountable public services. The well-being of our communities and societies depends on it (Eurodad, 2018, p. 5)

In line with the temper of the times, a series of tweets by Eurodad staff follow the Executive Summary to celebrate International Women's Day (https://www .eurodad.org/international_womens_day_2019, accessed March 2019) calling for:

- 'Economic justice, gender justice'
- 'By closing tax loopholes, and by tackling unsustainable debt and privat-ization of development finance, Eurodad's work contributes to ensuring sufficient public finance for quality and adequate public services in educa-tion, health and infrastructure. These are crucial ingredients for women's empowerment.'

While these statements seem unremarkable, the same cannot be said of the accompanying website that, without pointing to an explanation, draws PPPs into the story:

> Government support for PPPs runs counter to their Global Goals commitments to promote gender equality and to fulfil women's rights.
> Bit.ly/PPPgender
> #Economic Justice for #GenderJustice@FemnetProg@GAD_Network

to which is added:

> PPPs DON'T JUST FAIL TO ADDRESS GENDER INEQUALITY, THEY MAY
> ACTUALLY EXACERBATE IT.

This is an indication of how unpopular PPPs have become.

European Court of Auditors (ECA)

This special report is one of a series setting out the results of the ECA's
audits of EU policies and programmes. Like the CSO report above, it makes
its conclusions clear at the outset. Special Report 09/2018 is entitled *Public
Private Partnerships in the EU: Widespread Shortcomings and Limited
Benefits.* Unlike the CSO report, however, it is not just a single viewpoint that
is presented, for the document also contains the European Commission's right
of reply.

Table 1.2 outlines the 12 projects examined by the Auditors, who conclude
as follows:

> We found that, although PPPs have the potential to deliver faster policy implemen-
> tation and ensure good maintenance levels throughout their life-time, the audited
> EU-supported PPPs were not always effectively managed and did not provide
> adequate value-for-money. Potential benefits of the audited PPPs were often not
> achieved, as – similarly to traditionally procured projects – they were subject to
> delays, cost increases and under-use of project outcomes, resulting in 1.5 billion
> euro of inefficient and ineffective spending, out of which 0.4 billion euro EU funds.
> (ECA, 2018, p. 49)

In seven of the nine completed projects (three Greek motorways, two Spanish
motorways, two French ICT projects), delays ranged from 2 to 52 months and
cost increases were close to €1.5 billion. But this result is nothing new, at least
for the Greek motorways, upon which for brevity we focus, given the prior
experience in the construction of traditionally procured motorways in Greece.
For example, two existing sections of the Olympia motorway, measuring
a total of 82 km, took up to 20 years and 31 procurement procedures to build.
The upgrade of the 64 km long Elefsina–Korinthos section to a motorway
required 20 years (from 1986 to 2006) and was implemented through 21 traditional public procurement contracts. Similarly, the construction of the 10 km
long Patra bypass section as a motorway required 11 years (from 1991 to 2002)
and was undertaken through ten traditional public procurement contracts.

Before the Greek motorway projects were put out to tender (and they drew
bids from across the European Union), there was a traffic analysis, financial
analysis, technical analysis and legal analysis carried out by consultants

Table 1.2   PPP projects audited by European Court of Auditors

	Sector/Projects	Contract status and duration	Delay in months	Planned total project cost (in millions of euros)	Provisional total project cost (in millions of euros)	Additional cost borne by the public partner (in millions of euros)	% cost increase	Comments	EU support (in millions of euros)
	Greece								
1	Transport: Central Motorway E-65	30-year concession (until 2038) construction – ongoing	47	2375	1594	413	See comment	The provisional total cost is lower than the planned total cost due to a project scope reduction by 55%. However, the total cost per km increased by 47%.	647.6
2	Transport: Olympia Motorway	30-year concession (until 2038) construction – ongoing	37	2825	2619	678	See comment	The provisional total cost is lower than the planned total cost due to a project scope reduction by 45%. However, the total cost per km increased by 69%.	1012.4
3	Transport: Moreas Motorway	30-year concession (until 2038) construction – completed	52	1543	1791	84	See comment	The total cost per km increased by 16%.	328.6

	Sector/Projects	Contract status and duration	Delay in months	Planned total project cost (in millions of euros)	Provisional total project cost (in millions of euros)	Additional cost borne by the public partner (in millions of euros)	% cost increase	Comments	EU support (in millions of euros)
	Spain								
4	Transport: Motorway A-1	19-year concession (until 2026) construction – completed	24	475	633	158	33%	Required modifications in the planned works.	2.2
5	Transport: Motorway C-25	33-year concession (until 2044) construction – completed	14	695	838	144	21%	Required modifications in the planned works and contract renegotiation.	70.0
	Ireland								
6	Transport: N17/18 Motorway	25-year concession (until 2042) construction – ongoing	n/a	946	n/a	n/a	See comment	Project construction was ongoing at the time of the audit.	2.7
7	ICT: National Broadband Schemes	5, 7-year project agreement, construction – completed	0	223	169	n/a	See comment	The project generated less revenue than expected as compared to the original tender due to the significantly lower than expected customer uptake. This has also impacted the overall operational expenditure, decreasing the initially estimated project funding.	36.0

	Sector/Projects	Contract status and duration	Delay in months	Planned total project cost (in millions of euros)	Provisional total project cost (in millions of euros)	Additional cost borne by the public partner (in millions of euros)	% cost increase	Comments	EU support (in millions of euros)
8	ICT: Metropolitan Area Networks (MAN)	Up to 25 years from last MAN certification	n/a	117	84	n/a	See comment	Project scope reduced, 4.2% increase in the average cost per town covered. The cost figure excludes the operation and maintenance of the infrastructure, for which there is a separate contract, and contribution from local authorities.	42.1
	France								
9	ICT: Le numérique au service des Girondins	20 years (until 2029) construction – completed	16	146	143	–4	–2%	Construction of the infrastructure was completed on time, but there was a 16-month delay for the commissioning of the project due to administrative factors.	12.5

	Sector/Projects	Contract status and duration	Delay in months	Planned total project cost (in millions of euros)	Provisional total project cost (in millions of euros)	Additional cost borne by the public partner (in millions of euros)	% cost increase	Comments	EU support (in millions of euros)
10	ICT: SPTHD Communauté de l'agglomération de Pau Pyrénées	15 years (until 2018) construction – ongoing	n/a	18	31	13	73%	Project construction was ongoing at the time of the audit. 73% cost increase in order to comply with introduced regulatory changes.	7.7
11	ICT: Proximite broadband in Meurthe et Moselle	26 years (until 2034) construction – completed	2	148	148	0	0%		5.9
12	ICT: Haute Pyrénées numérique	22 years (until 2031) construction – completed	0	107	106	–1	–1%		0.9
	Total			**9618**	**8156**	**1490**			**2169**

Source: ECA (2018).

selected under an open and competitive selection procedure. According to the Commission, these analyses led to the conclusion that the only viable option to complete the Trans-European Transport Network (TEN) motorway network projects in Greece over a ten-year horizon was to combine available EU and national resources with private funds. The Auditors' report noted the absence of a Public Sector Comparator (PSC), to which the Commission replied that,

> in light of the chronic failure of the traditional public procurement the PSC would not have had any value added on the decision to structure the motorway concessions contracts in Greece. Both delays observed in traditional public works contracts and the lack of sufficient financial resources advocate for the PPP solution. (Ibid., p. 6)

As it turned out, the switch to PPP and the involvement of private finance proved to be no panacea. But the circumstances at the time were not propitious. A lot of the cost changes and delays can likely be attributed to:

> difficulties in the markets under the stress of the 2008 GFC crisis, not necessarily to the PPPs process *per se*, exacerbated by the collapse in traffic volumes (63 per cent Central, 40 per cent Olympia, and 20 per cent Moreas) as pan-European trade was hit and economic activity declined.

In conclusion, and considering all the evidence, the European Commission acknowledges that 'PPPs are more complex than purely public projects' (ibid., p. 2). From a reading of the Auditors' report a number of reasons for this view can be discerned:

- protracted procurement
- construction delays
- authorization delays
- legal disputes
- renegotiations
- difficulties reaching financial close
- vulnerability to changing financial and economic conditions, gold-plating ('affordability illusions')
- bad traffic forecasts
- poor risk sharing.

CONCLUDING REMARKS

Again, there is nothing new in this listing. Nor is it peculiar to PPPs. Rather, the complexity is inherent in infrastructure itself and its procurement. Nevertheless, having said that, the combined weight of the abandonment of PFI by the government that pioneered PPPs, the single-minded indictment of PPPs in the CSO report, and the report of the ECA on PPPs ('widespread shortcomings and limited benefits') makes for disturbing reading. All in all, it seems a compelling reason and an opportune time for rethinking PPPs.

NOTES

1. There are many different types of PPPs, as will be made clear as this volume unfolds. In particular, the bundled project-specific PPP, which for the most part is the focus in this book, differs from partnerships created for policy formulation. Very different again are those used historically for colonization. For example, in a UK Channel 5 programme *Portillo's Empire Journey*, Michael Portillo described the relationship between the British government and the East India Company in the governance of India, based on monopoly trading rights and a private army, as a public private partnership. In similar vein, I described the role of the private South Australian Company in the formation of the Colony of South Australia as a form of public private partnership (Lewis, 2001).
2. Quite why this was so has never been understandable to me. One possibility is opposition to private sector involvement in public services. Having lost the battle over privatization and contracting out, there may have been a determination to prevent further private sector encroachment into the delivery of public services.

2.   How did the idea of PPPs arise?

THE SWINGING PENDULUM

From where did public private partnerships (PPPs) and the idea of private financing and operation of infrastructure come? At one level, the answer is very simple. The idea is not a new one. Toll roads and toll bridges have been around since antiquity. In Britain and the United States in the eighteenth and nineteenth centuries, over two and a half thousand companies were chartered and incorporated to develop private turnpikes (i.e. roads). They in turn came under competitive pressures from the next private infrastructure development – the railways. PPP-type arrangements have been used in France to privately finance public infrastructure since the seventeenth century, when the French concession model was pioneered. In the second half of the nineteenth century, France extensively used concessions to finance its infrastructure development. Railways, water, electricity and tramways were all designed, constructed, financed and operated by private enterprises and banks.

This rich history of private involvement in infrastructure was, at the same time, a chequered one. By way of illustration consider the London Underground, the world's first electric tube. Each of the companies engaged in the building of the seven underground lines between 1894 and 1907 first had to be chartered by means of a Private Act of Parliament, then capital had to be raised, rights of way negotiated, and the construction undertaken (normally over four years). Those travelling on the 'tube' today may wonder why there are long straight sections followed by sudden changes of direction. This is because the railway companies found it easier to negotiate rights of way with one or two authorities than with each of the many individual property owners above the line. Consequently, the lines were built to follow below ground the course of the streets and roads above. Further, some of the companies had great difficulties in raising the necessary capital,[1] and a number of rationalizations eventually saw ownership of the lines concentrated in two hands. The financial difficulties of the companies stemmed from two sources, one technological, the other regulatory. These two factors – technological improvements and regulatory changes – plague and thus pose threats to any transport infrastructure investment.

In terms of technology, when the companies obtained their charters and began construction, petrol-driven buses broke down frequently and could not withstand the rigours of everyday use and constant stopping and starting in heavy traffic. They appeared to pose little potential threat to underground trains. By the time the underground system finally had been put in place in 1907, buses were more reliable. The X-type and improved B-type motor buses introduced in 1909 and 1910 respectively could average 12 mph and, with the advantage of running on public roads, operated at considerable profits while the underground lines were struggling to make money.

Trams provided the other source of competition. While overhead trains were excluded from the grid formed by the Metropolitan and District lines, a change to the regulatory environment allowed electric trams, some private, others municipal (e.g. London County Council), to operate within the 'inner circuit' or 'circle'. London County Council electric tramcars were allowed to cross Westminster Bridge and run along the Victoria Embankment for the first time on 15 December 1906.

On both scores, by the time they were built the underground railway lines faced competition from two sources, neither of which had been anticipated in their business forecasts. While some of the companies provided steady returns, most of the private shareholders probably breathed a sigh of relief when the underground rail companies were effectively nationalized with compensation when the London Passenger Transport Board, a public corporation, took over operations in July 1933, and risks passed to the Board and the public purse.

Much the same story unfolded as turnpikes were replaced by railways, and later railways by motorways and passenger liners by airlines. The private ventures made significant contributions to the improvement of transport infrastructure, but the companies themselves (or more correctly, the shareholders) faced serious risks. Their financial viability was vulnerable to competition from new technological advances, and to changes in the rules of the regulatory game. Thereafter, public provision and financing was dominant for most of the twentieth century as governments became the principal providers of infrastructure (at least outside of the United States), but in recent decades, private financing has returned to being, if not quite the top, certainly an important part of the agenda, so exemplifying the observation of Vives et al. (2010) that 'throughout history the provision of infrastructure services has been like a swinging pendulum, going between pure public provision to pure private provision' (p. 412).

Having made this significant point, those authors then proceed to qualify it in an important way, arguing that the public–private dichotomy is too sharp and ultimately unhelpful:

> [I]n every infrastructure service provision there will inevitably be public and private participation. All projects are therefore a public–private partnership (PPP) where

all infrastructure investments involve the public and the private sectors, and some partnership between them. Private enterprises or individuals will be involved; either as users, suppliers, contractors, or stakeholders in one way or another. The public sector will also be involved, be it as provider of services or at the very least, in a regulatory capacity, as infrastructure is considered a public service. (Ibid., p. 412)

No longer was the norm a relatively clear separation of the public sector and the private sector in the provision of public infrastructure services. There was disenchantment with public sector services, marked by a monopoly position and the absence of competition. Also, there was a lack of choice, little innovation and little accountability to customers, along with political interference, especially with budgets. Thus the public sector was viewed as inefficient and burdened with excessive bureaucracy. Perhaps, as Rosenau (2000, p. 4) put it, the introduction of the private sector could deliver better quality at lower cost. As a result, the situation began to change. Faced with budgetary stringencies and, at the same time, pressure to expand and improve public facilities and services, governments turned to the private sector, in order to harness private resources and achieve better value for money. Private sector entities have entered into long-term contractual agreements to construct or manage public sector infrastructure facilities, or to provide services to the community (using the infrastructure facilities built). In these ways, the private sector was given more responsibility for the delivery of public services.

Such changes do not occur in a policy vacuum. While there may be pressures from the ground up for change, invariably some intellectual structure or conceptual framework is sought as a support. This leads us to the research on PPPs.

RESEARCH ON PPPS

Marsilio et al. (2011) examine the intellectual structure of research into PPPs, by tabulating and classifying published works on the topic using academic citations. In their words,

> citation analysis aims to identify the works and authors that have had a significant impact on a field of academic research (impact indicators). It is based on the principle that authors cite documents and authors they consider to be important for the development of their research; the most frequently cited documents and authors are likely to exert more influence than those who are less frequently cited. (p. 766)

In this case, the PPP research was identified using the well-known ISI Web of Science database, the Social Sciences Citation Index (SSCI), by entering two key words, namely public private partnership (PPP) and public private collaboration (PPC). As the authors say, 'these key words are often used to identify

Table 2.1   *Most cited documents in PPP research*

Rank	Raw freq. > 4	Document cited	Book/Journal
1	10	Savas (2000)	B
2	7	Osborne (2000)	B
3	7	Osborne and Gaebler (1993)	B
4	7	Linder (1999)	J
5	7	Grimsey and Lewis (2004b)	B
6	7	Buse and Walt (2000a)	J
7	6	Uplekar et al. (1998)	J
8	6	Rosenau (2000)	J
9	6	Buse and Waxman (2001)	J
10	6	Buse and Walt (2000b)	J
11	5	Williamson (1985)	B
12	5	Uplekar et al. (2001)	J
13	5	Porter (1990)	B
14	5	Logan and Molotch (1987)	B
15	5	Grout (1997)	J
16	5	Batley (1996)	J

Source: Marsilio et al. (2011).

institutional collaborations between the public and private sector' (p. 757). The authors consider 1990 to be the effective starting date for the PPP literature. Hence the time frame for the bibliometric analysis is 18 years from 1990 to 2007, and the final database includes 323 references.

Considering the classifications, surprisingly, most (94 per cent) of the authors have published just one work on PPPs. In terms of author affiliation, the most cited authors are the World Health Organization and the World Bank, followed by economist Oliver Williamson (writing on transactions cost). The most preferred journals for publication are in healthcare and public administration. Had the study been extended beyond 2007, it seems likely that public policy scholars would feature more prominently, especially the writings of Graeme Hodge and Carsten Greve (2005, 2017, 2019).

The other classification is the one which seems most relevant for the issue under examination, namely, how did PPPs arise, enter the literature and shape research and policy analysis? This alternative classification group catalogues the most cited documents. Table 2.1 sets out the 16 most cited documents identified by Marsilio et al. For our purposes, and to save space, we will focus on the five most cited works, in the order that they are listed. Interestingly, four of the five works are books, which somewhat runs against the tide in academia today.

SAVAS (2000)

Emanuel Savas is an unabashed advocate of privatization, a theme first pursued in *Privatizing the Public Sector: How to Shrink Government* (1982), and then *Privatization: The Key to Better Government* (1987) and *Privatization and Public–Private Partnerships* (2000). Savas is proud to acknowledge an intellectual heritage going back to Milton Friedman, Gordon Tullock, Anthony Downs, William Niskanen and Peter Drucker. Interestingly, however, his conversion to the merits of privatization owed little to them. Rather, he was persuaded to the case for what he termed 'prudent privatization' by his time in government and 'what I have learned in thirty years of experience with numerous state and local governments, the federal government, and in forty-seven countries' (2000, p. xv).

An article in *Harper's Magazine* in 1971 ('Municipal Monopoly') marked Savas's first published venture into the topic. In it he argued that the issue was not public versus private but monopoly versus competition, calling for more competition in public services. From there it was a short step to regard 'contracting with the private sector as an obvious way to introduce much-needed competition into the delivery of public services, reinvigorate public agencies, and break up malfunctioning municipal monopolies that more often than not (at least in New York) were controlled by public-employee unions rather than by public officials' (2000, p. xv). The 2000 book sought to go one step further, treating privatization not as an abstract concept, but as a pragmatic strategy for improving how government operates, as illustrated by the following:

- It is a fallacy that privatization is anti-people and lacking the compassion thought to be inherent in government programmes. Indeed, people are harmed by badly run government programmes.
- The purpose of privatization is to improve government performance and thereby improve the lives of those who are most reliant on government. Saving money and enhancing services for all taxpayers improves their lives as well.
- Private non-profit organizations run better homeless shelters at lower cost than does government.
- Opponents cite mismanagement and corruption in private firms. There are badly run private firms, but the same ills can be found also in government agencies.
- Poorly performing private firms tend to go out of business, while poorly performing public agencies are often given more money to try to overcome their shortcomings.

Savas took aim at a number of (some may say easy) targets:

> The principal reason why privatization leads to greater efficiency is not lower wages and benefits but greater productivity, that is, fewer workers needed to do the same amount of work. (Ibid., p. 287)

> ... workers facing the prospect of privatization have two fears: some are afraid they will have no work, while others are afraid they will have to work. (Ibid., p. 289)

> ... social services have long been contracted out to the private sector – to nonprofit organizations. This has been a 'fatal embrace', because private, nonprofit organizations with distinguished histories have become, in effect, government surrogates subject to coercive regulations that sap their initiative and thwart their efforts to find better ways to help the needy; they have lost their independence in the scramble for government dollars.

> ... evidence mounts that for-profit firms can deliver equally high-quality services more cost-effectively than nonprofits.

> ... The ideological ethos and the anti-market, anti-profit bias of the social-services professions, however, often combined with holier-than-thou attitudes, have blinded the non-profit establishment, just as government officials thirty years ago scoffed at the notion that for-profit private firms could undersell and outperform non-profit government agencies. (Ibid., p. 324)

> To a misguided few, the very word *privatize* summons forth images from emotional depths and causes misunderstanding and polarization. (Ibid., p. 299)

> Some tend to read into privatization a plot to establish a completely free market, with overtones of dog-eat-dog, survival of the fittest, and culling of the weakest. Others interpret the word as an attack on government, government programs, and direct beneficiaries of government programs, including employees; therefore they defend these interests by attacking privatization. Still others are provoked by the term because they see it as an attack on the ideals they cherish: *public* to them denotes brotherhood, sharing, caring, and community, and they interpret *private* to mean abandoning these vital values. (Ibid., p. 300)

So far we have not discussed exactly what is meant by privatization. In Britain and many Commonwealth countries (Australia, Canada, New Zealand) it means what Mrs Thatcher, British Prime Minister from 1979 to 1990, was doing, that is, selling off public assets such as nationalized industries to private sector entities such as private sector corporations or the sale of council houses to tenants, and customers of utilities becoming shareholders. From an American perspective the net is cast a little wider.

> Privatization can be defined broadly as relying more on the private institutions of society and less on government to satisfy people's needs. It is the act of reducing the role of government or increasing the role of the other institutions of society in producing goods and services and in owning property. In general, both the public

and private sectors play important roles, and it is increasingly common to refer to 'public–private partnerships', a less contentious term than 'privatization.' A public–private partnership is defined as an arrangement between a government and the private sector in which ... traditionally public activities are performed by the private sector. (Ibid., pp. 3–4)

Given as examples, although there are many more, are:

- contracting out rubbish collection, maintaining government buildings, processing claims, and repairing military aircraft;
- awarding franchises to build, operate and/or maintain bridges, tunnels and so on;
- issuing food stamps, housing vouchers or educational vouchers;
- volunteer fire fighting, neighbourhood security patrols;
- government stops running bus services or providing home insurance;
- selling or leasing government railroads, factories.

Consequently, to Savas, PPPs take on three roles. First, the term partnership enables government bodies to avoid using more contentious descriptions such as privatization or contracting out. Ironically, the term PPP has since become equally unpopular. Second, PPP embraces a wide range of public–private interactions in the provision of public services. Third, the use of PPPs for infrastructure procurement has become almost a distinctive field of its own, with bundling analysis, complex contracting, risk evaluation and risk allocation generating an extensive literature.

In ending this review of Savas, there are a few things on which he can be challenged. One is his contention that poorly performing private firms can simply be allowed to go out of business. Admittedly, anyone dealing with a private enterprise faces the possibility that it can go bankrupt. For someone buying breakfast cereal that risk may not matter a great deal, as there are close substitutes available. For a private firm providing public services the consequences may be less benign and create considerable disruption for vulnerable groups relying on the services. Suppliers or contractors can be replaced eventually, but at a cost to customers and to the public sector entity that must take up the slack, perhaps at short notice. Such considerations do not rule out contracting out or privatization, although it does imply that government needs to conduct regular financial checks on the partners. Such a governance framework is outlined in Grimsey and Lewis (2004a).

Another matter concerns competition. On performance and efficiency grounds, Savas, in the quotation given earlier, argues the centrality of injecting much needed competition into the delivery of public services, and sees contracting out or privatization as a means of doing so. This ignores the role of potential competition over actual competition. Wholesale privatization of public services generates fierce resistance from public service unions and suspicions from the anti-market lobby groups. An alternative is to rely on 'contestability' and the often unstated, while credible, threat that the work of the government department could be outsourced if productivity gains are not achieved.

Finally, on a number of occasions Savas stated that privatization is on the ascendant (2000, p. 328) and that the trend is 'unmistakably' away from government and towards other institutional forms embraced by privatization (including PPPs) in line with what was called earlier 'the swinging pendulum' of public and private involvement in public services and infrastructure build-ing. Instead, under the banner of 'millennial socialism', millennials – espe-cially on campus – exhibit a widespread mistrust of markets and call loudly for a green-left socialist agenda. They believe:

> that inequality has spiralled out of control and that the economy is rigged in favour of vested interests. They believe that the public yearns for income and power to be redistributed by the state to balance the scales. They think that myopia and lobbying have led governments to ignore the increasing likelihood of climate catastrophe. And they believe that the hierarchies which govern society and the economy – regu-lators, bureaucracies and companies – no longer serve the interests of ordinary folk and must be 'democratised'. (The Economist, 2019a, p. 9)

> Much of what the centre left thought in the 1990s and 2000s has been abandoned, not just by vanguardist millennial socialists, but by a broad swathe of left-wing opinion. The median supporter of left-wing parties is increasingly sceptical about free trade, averse to foreign wars and distrustful of public–private partnerships. What they still like is the income redistribution that came with those policies. They want higher minimum wages and a lot more spending on public services. (The Economist, 2019b, p. 17)

Savas can hardly be held to account for not having foreseen these develop-ments, although it is the case that university faculty and students have been moving to the left for several decades, culminating in a situation where voices other than the radical left struggle to be heard. There is no doubt, moreover, that he underestimated the power that public sector unions can continue to exercise, as well as what he called 'the anti-market, anti-profit bias of the social service professionals'.

STEPHEN OSBORNE (2000) (EDITED VOLUME)

Unlike the others, this study is an edited volume with 20 different contribu-tions, drawing on examples, case studies and practices from 21 countries, along with the United Nations and World Bank. As such, it encompasses a wide variety of PPPs in various areas of public policy and administration (listed below), illustrating how versatile the concept of partnership is, and how it has been employed in almost every aspect of social and economic policy:

- industry development, economic regeneration, urban environment, urban renewal, slum clearance, harbour development;
- social welfare, healthcare, social housing, hospital services, childcare, old-age care, services for handicapped, poverty alleviation;
- labour relations, immigration services, trade, microeconomic reform, land acquisition, business attraction;
- manufacturing networks, environmental improvements, technological innovation, knowledge development, rural development support services, English-language training;
- public transport, public parks, refuse collection.

All these partnership arrangements for these applications feature in the volume.

In order to encompass this diverse range of activities, a number of definitions of PPPs are offered. In fact, seven definitions are provided over the space of one page alone in the chapter by Ronald McQuaid on 'The Theory of Partnerships' (pp. 10–11):

1. Partnership involves cooperation – that is, 'to work or act together' – and in a public policy can be defined as cooperation between people or organizations in the public or private sector for mutual benefit (see Holland, 1984).
2. Harding (1998) sets out a similar general definition of 'private–public partnership' as 'any action which relies on the agreement of actors in the public and private sectors and which also contributes in some way to improving the urban economy and the quality of life'.
3. Taking an economic development perspective, Sellgren (1990) defines partnership as a scheme with involvement or funding from more than one agency.
4. Bailey (1994) provides a working definition of private–public partnership in urban regeneration as 'the mobilisation of a coalition of interests drawn from more than one sector in order to prepare and oversee an agreed strategy for regeneration of a defined area' (p. 293).
5. Bennett and Krebs (1994) similarly stress the joint objectives of the bodies and defines partnership as cooperation between actors where they agree to work together towards a specified economic-development objective and draw the key distinction between generalized policy communities that develop a broad local vision for the area or local economy and the specific networks (or partnerships) that are necessary to support individual projects.

6. The UK government has defined the partnership approach as involving the 'voluntary commitment by the wide range of bodies with a contribution to make to urban development or regeneration (including local communities, the local authorities, government departments and agencies and the private sector) to an agreed comprehensive long-term regeneration strategy for their areas' (The Scottish Office, 1993, p. 6).

7. Atkinson (1999) argues that there are varying meanings of words such as partnerships and the meaning assigned to partnership in urban and rural regeneration in the UK is an exercise in power which reinforces social relations.

Since any combination of the public sector, the private sector and non-government organizations (NGOs) is liable to be called a partnership, elsewhere in the book there are a number of important corollaries. In particular, a partnership needs to be an 'authentic partnership' (p. 316), and not just a 'buzzword to sprinkle liberally through any funding application in order to improve its chances of success' (p. 327). Often in the PPP literature a clear distinction is made between policy formulation and policy implementation, with the government 'presumed to maintain control over policy formulation whilst a plurality of providers were invited into the domain of service provision under a contract providing the core governance mechanism for regulating relationships between the so-called partners' (p. 326). By contrast, a 'true' partnership is one which 'cuts across the established policy making–implementation divide' (p. 326), based on improving participation and a sharing of skills, knowledge and learning (p. 316).

Such partnerships, by involving both development and delivery, would, it is claimed, create extra value due to cooperation (p. 91), resulting in new solutions based on an exchange of information and ideas (p. 92), thereby achieving something that could not have eventuated without the collaboration (p. 293). If this is so, the result could be a better sharing and more efficient use of resources (p. 316), and greater public legitimacy for policy when there is local participation and less top-down activity employing command and control authority (p. 21).

Finally, in the concluding chapter by McLaughlin and Osborne, five challenges are identified in any attempt to move to a system of what is called 'public governance' or 'community governance' that revolves around the interdependency of the actors in policy formulation networks (p. 332). The first challenge is that this type of partnership must be understood as a 'process rather than as a document or structure' (p. 333). Second, values need to change in the move from a service agency to a policymaking partnership. Third, the role of politicians has to transform from 'being the sole sources of policy initiatives ... towards being facilitators and supporters' (p. 333). Fourth, in the process local governments must necessarily cede some part of their powers to voluntary and community organizations when engaging in partnerships with the voluntary, non-profit sector. Fifth, for plural policymaking to work local governments must commit to building the capacity of the non-profit sector to participate in planning and implementation. In much the same way, private sector participants in central government PPPs have acquired additional skills and knowledge, achieving something that may not have eventuated without collaboration (p. 293). This concept of 'collaborative advantage' – that is, the advantage to be gained when members of one organization act collaboratively with members of another organization, thereby realizing things that could not otherwise be obtained – is regarded as the ultimate goal of all partnership initiatives.

Usefully, these themes are explored further in the volume, with many valuable insights especially about the preconditions for a partnership. First, however hackneyed the expression is, there needs to be the potential for synergy of some form, so 'the sum is greater than the parts'. Second, the partnership involves both development and delivery of a strategy or a set of projects or operations, although each actor may not be equally involved in all stages. Third, in public–private partnerships the public sector are not pursuing purely commercial goals, and thus the partnership must embrace non-financial benefits as well as commercial transactions (p. 11).

Also, there is the question of what can be expected to be attained from the partnership. One is the creation of extra value due to cooperation. Another is new solutions, based on the exchange of information and ideas, and the sharing of skills, knowledge and learning. The hoped-for synergy requires that the partners trust one another (p. 87).

OSBORNE AND GAEBLER (1993)

This 'national best seller', carrying a cover endorsement by Bill Clinton, is written by David Osborne, author and journalist, and Ted Gaebler, a former city manager of Visalia, California. Their central thesis is that the problems faced by governments at all levels (federal, state and local) will not be solved by spending more or spending less, by creating new public bureaucracies or by privatizing existing bureaucracies. Instead, governments have to be made effective by reinventing themselves. Osborne and Gaebler contend that the central failure of government is one of means, not ends, and their subject is not what governments do, but how they operate.

The authors begin their story with what they term 'industrial-era governments', with their large centralized bureaucracies and standardized 'one-size-fits-all' services. As they note, for a long time the bureaucratic model worked, not because it was efficient, but because it solved the basic problems people wanted solved. It provided security from unemployment and during old age. It provided stability, a particularly important quality after the Great Depression. It provided a basic sense of fairness and equity. It provided jobs. And it delivered the basic, no-frills, one-size-fits-all services people wanted and expected during the industrial era: roads, motorways, water, sewers, schools, postal services.

In short, during times of crisis – the Great Depression and two world wars – the bureaucratic model worked well. When goals were clear and widely shared, when tasks were relatively straightforward, and when most were willing to pitch in for the cause, the top-down, command-and-control ethos got things done.

Conditions have now changed and, with them, so has the business and economic environment. We operate in an information and knowledge-based society, and the marketplace is global. This is true of government as well as private firms. Most government institutions perform increasingly complex tasks, in competitive, rapidly changing environs, with customers who want quality and choice in public education, public healthcare and public housing. As service demands increased and revenue sources declined, governments had no choice under this fiscal pressure but to change the way that they did business. Officials embraced PPPs and developed alternative ways to deliver public services.

To this end, Osborne and Gaebler outline ten principles. Governments should (1) steer, not row (as 'it is not government's obligation to provide services, but to see that they're provided'); (2) empower communities to solve their own problems rather than simply deliver services; (3) encourage competition rather than monopolies; (4) be driven by missions, rather than rules; (5) be results-oriented by funding outcomes rather than inputs; (6) meet the needs of the customer not the bureaucracy; (7) concentrate on earning money rather than spending it; (8) invest in preventing problems rather than curing crises; (9) decentralize authority; and (10) solve problems by influencing market forces rather than creating public programmes.

In the authors' words,

> Most entrepreneurial governments [the term for governments that follow their ten principles] promote competition between service providers. They empower citizens by pushing control out of the bureaucracy, into the community. They measure the performance of their agencies, focusing not on inputs but on outcomes. They are driven by their goals – their missions – not by their rules and regulations. They redefine their clients as customers and offer them choices – between schools, between training programs, between housing options. They prevent problems before they emerge, rather than simply offering services afterward. They put their energies into earning money, not simply spending it. They decentralize authority, embracing participatory management. They prefer market mechanisms to bureaucratic mech-

anisms. And they focus not simply on providing public services, but on catalyzing all sectors – public, private, and voluntary – into action to solve their community's problems. (Osborne and Gaebler, 1993, pp. 19–20)

Privatization is seen by Osborne and Gaebler as *one* answer, but not *the* answer, privatization being understood as actions abandoning many governmental functions to the private sector, selling others, and contracting with private firms to handle others. The authors go on:

> Services can be contracted out or turned over to the private sector. But governance cannot. We can privatize discrete steering functions, but not the overall process of governance. If we did, we would have no mechanism by which to make collective decisions, no way to set the rules of the marketplace, no means to enforce rules of behavior. We would lose all sense of equity and altruism: services that could not generate a profit, whether housing for the homeless or health care for the poor, would barely exist. Third sector organizations could never shoulder the entire load.
>
> Business does some things better than government, but government does some things better than business. The public sector tends to be better, for instance, at policy management, regulation, ensuring equity, preventing discrimination or exploitation, ensuring continuity and stability of services, and ensuring social cohesion (through the mixing of races and classes, for example, in the public schools). (Ibid., pp. 45–6)

It makes sense to put the delivery of many public services in private hands (whether for-profit or non-profit) if by so doing a government can get more effectiveness, efficiency, equity or accountability. But we should not mistake this transfer for some grand ideology of privatizing government. When governments contract with private businesses, both conservatives and liberals often talk as if they are shifting a fundamental public responsibility to the private sector. Osborne and Gaebler say that this is nonsense. They are shifting the delivery of services, not the responsibility for services. The fact that a road is built by a private contractor does not make the road a private road. When governments contract activities to the private sector, those governments still take the policy decisions and provide the financing.

By way of concluding this summary of Osborne and Gaebler, two points can be made. First, some of their arguments made on the grounds of equity and social cohesion would raise the hackles of free-marketeers or libertarians. For example, the authors see one of the desirable outcomes of public education being that children are given the chance to rub elbows with others from many walks of life, so making democracy work (ibid., p. 46). Discussion of such issues lead to the 'old saw' of the core or essential role of government in a market economy. Second, in terms of policy formulation, there is the question of what role the private sector can play in formulating (as opposed to delivering) policy, and thus participating in so-called public private policy partnerships (Rosenau, 2000).

STEPHEN LINDER (1999)

In his article 'Coming to Terms with the Public–Private Partnership', Linder defines a public private partnership as 'a rubric for describing cooperative ventures between the state and private business' (1999, p. 35). The article appeared in the *American Behavioural Scientist* along with an introductory piece by Pauline Rosenau in a special issue of the journal. Later in 2000, an edited book by Rosenau (2000), titled *Public–Private Policy Partnerships* (#8 in Table 2.1), reprinted Linder (1999) in its entirety, and includes an introductory chapter written by Linder and Rosenau, 'Mapping the Terrain of the Public–Private Policy Partnership'. In these ways, the two studies are intertwined.

In Linder and Rosenau (2000), partnerships are described as the 'second generation' of efforts to bring competitive market forces to bear on government provision of goods and services. The 'first generation' took the form of privatization of public services embracing 'deregulation, policy decentralization, downsizing of government, outsourcing of public services and privatization of sectors previously assumed to be what economists called natural monopolies, including gas, electricity, telephone, and so forth' (ibid., pp. 5–6). As distinct from the first generation of privatizing efforts, 'partnering involves a sharing of both responsibility and financial risk' (ibid., p. 9).

Linder takes up the story from there in his article. Partnerships are frequently viewed as a derivative of the drive to privatize, but this lineage is questioned. Public asset sales, outsourcing (e.g. procurement contracts) and local shedding (e.g. divestiture) that occurred in these regimes was nominally intended to bring discipline to the provision of services through competitive market pressures. The rationale was that private providers would provide higher-quality goods and services at lower cost, and the government sector of public providers would shrink accordingly vis-à-vis the market. By contrast, the hallmark of partnerships is cooperation, not competition. The disciplining mechanism is not customer exit or thin profit margins, but a cooperative arrangement that spreads financial risks between public and private sectors. According to Linder, such joint-venture arrangements actually stabilize volatile markets and work to mitigate competitive pressures, not exploit them. Rather than struggling to redefine the boundary between public and private, with the former typically ceding territory to the latter, partnering works to blur the two. Public and private are not separated but brought together in a productive way.

Drawing on the US experience, Linder (1999, pp. 41–8) suggests six ways in which PPPs can introduce change into the public sector. First, PPPs are a tool for management reform. As such, PPPs can alter the way government functions by introducing market disciplines into public services. Second, PPPs encourage problem conversion, so that the task for public sector managers becomes one of reframing constraints they face so as to facilitate the entry of private sector operators and their commitment of funds. The focus becomes one of the outcomes to be achieved, rather than the processes by which things are done. Third, once this is done, PPPs can produce a 'moral regeneration' by widening the number of stakeholders in the outcome and building market experience for public service managers. Fourth, PPPs allow for financial risks to be shifted from public to private investors. Fifth, partnerships can be a vehicle for restructuring public services, streamlining administrative procedures and substituting a private workplace for public workers. Sixth, as power-sharing arrangements, PPPs can alter business–government relations in fundamental ways. One is that an ethos of cooperation and trust can replace the adversarial relations endemic to command-and-control regulation. Also, any relationship between partners will involve some mutually beneficial sharing of responsibility, knowledge or risk. In most instances, each party brings something of value to the others to be invested or exchanged. Finally, there is an expectation of give-and-take between partners, negotiating differences that were otherwise litigated. To Linder, this aspect is the essence of partnerships.

GRIMSEY AND LEWIS (2004B)

What did Darrin Grimsey and I have in mind by a PPP? Since any relationship involving some combination of the private, voluntary and public sectors is prone to be labelled a 'partnership', it may be useful to define what a partnership is in this particular context. PPPs can be defined as arrangements whereby private parties participate in, or provide support for, the provision of infrastructure, and a PPP project results in a contract for a private entity to deliver public infrastructure-based services.

A defining feature of a PPP is that the public sector does not buy an asset; it is purchasing a stream of services under specified terms and conditions. This aspect is the key to the viability (or not) of the transaction since it is designed to provide the right economic incentives. Basic elements of the PPP model to which most attention was given by Grimsey and me are as follows:

- The public sector defines the services it requires over a long-term period (typically 15–30 years) by reference to an output specification and closely specified performance criteria, without being too prescriptive about the means of delivery.

- No payments are made until the asset is delivered and working, and subsequent payments are subject to reduction if service performance standards are not met.
- Design risk, in terms of the decision on the nature of assets required to deliver the services to the necessary standard, is left to the private sector entity and the assets are effectively owned and operated by the private sector for the duration of the arrangement.
- The public sector provides no funding during the construction phase, and the risk of cost overruns, delays, and so on reside with the private sector.
- The public sector has to devolve control to the private sector over the assets and resources needed to deliver the service to such an extent that the private sector bears the risks and receives the rewards of effective ownership.

Not everyone agrees with that definition. Others would suggest that the emphasis on asset-based infrastructure is too narrowly based, and would define PPPs much more broadly. For example, in Table 1.2, Grimsey and I gave some details of PPPs in the United States. PPPs have covered transport (e.g. toll roads) and private prisons and detention facilities, but have also dealt with education policy priority setting, welfare provision, health and medical services, and a range of community activities and services from schooling to urban regeneration and environmental policy. This broader framework encompasses both 'policy-level' partnerships and 'project-level' partnerships. Policy-level partnerships coordinate public sector and private sector inputs into decision-making about the design and formulation of policy initiatives. In the case of transportation, for example, policy-level partnerships evaluate the various modes of transport, and develop general rules for operation, investment and the resolution of disputes. Project-level partnerships, by contrast, focus on specific sites or situations, such as the establishment of a new urban transit terminal, with the aim of drawing private capital and management into the project. Policy-level and project-level partnerships have always gone hand in hand in the United States, but this has not always been the case elsewhere.

The reconciliation between these two views of PPPs turns in part on how 'infrastructure' is defined. Many of the apparent differences disappear once allowance is made for the variety of forms that infrastructure can take, in particular the distinction between 'economic' and 'social', and 'hard' and 'soft' (see Table 2.2). When PPPs began in the UK (and Australia), they were largely applied to 'economic' areas like motorways, bridges, tunnels and so on. Then they were used for government office accommodation, hospitals, schools, prisons and so on. Next came social housing, urban regeneration and waste management. New integrated ways of delivering healthcare and other community services were explored. In addition, there are partnerships for

Table 2.2   *Classification of infrastructure by type*

	Hard	Soft
Economic	roads	vocational training
	motorways	financial institutions
	bridges	R&D facilitation
	ports	technology transfer
	railways	export assistance
	airports	
	telecommunications	
	power	
Social	hospitals	social security
	schools	community services
	water supply	environmental protection agencies
	housing	(EPAs)
	sewerage	
	childcare	
	prisons	
	aged care homes	

Source: Grimsey and Lewis (2004b), p. 21.

heritage sites, estates and facilities management, and a 'green' agenda has been overlaid. This evolution again shows the adaptability of the concept.

THE DEVELOPMENT OF PPPS

Having considered various definitions covering the scope of PPPs, it is time to address the subject title of this chapter and seek an answer to the question of how PPPs came into being. In 2004 Darrin Grimsey and I saw that the PPP concept had been aided by ideas in a number of fields that had coalesced to inform the arrangement, notably:

- the changing environment for public services;
- dissatisfaction with traditional procurement;
- development of the private financing model.

In parallel with writing the 2004 volume, we put together a collection of 36 articles that shaped our thinking, which was published the next year (Grimsey and Lewis, 2005a). Two of the articles bear directly on the three influences. These are Hood (1995 [2005a]) and Hodgson (1995 [2005a]). Consider, first, the contribution of Hood. PPPs can be seen as part of a broad shift in the workings of government and the search for new forms of governance, under what became known as 'new public management'. Hood's article considers the various dimensions of 'new public management' as follows: (1) a shift towards greater disaggregation of public organizations into separately managed 'corporatized units'; (2) a shift towards greater competition both between public sector organizations and between public sector organizations and the private sector; (3) a move towards greater use within the public sector of private sector management practices; (4) an active search for finding alternative, less costly ways to deliver public services; (5) a move towards more 'hands on management'; (6) a move towards more explicit and measurable standards of performance; and (7) attempts to control public organizations according to preset output measures.

Corporatization, privatization, commercialization, managerialism, outsourcing and downsizing of public sector activities can be seen as consequences of the new public management movement. But so, too, in a very different way are PPPs because they enable public services to be provided by public and private sector entities working in partnership. In order to appreciate where PPPs fit into all of this, it is useful to consider the broad range of public sector business models for public infrastructure that have been spawned by these developments and that have widened the interface between public and private agencies.

Implementation of this agenda has spawned a number of different public sector business models, and widened the interface between public and private agencies. Box 2.1 sets out a veritable alphabet soup of public/private business models, starting from complete public provision ('collectivization') at one

---

BOX 2.1   THE 'ALPHABET SOUP' OF INFRASTRUCTURE PUBLIC–PRIVATE BUSINESS MODELS

TRADITIONAL APPROACHES

- Public provision and supply of collective goods
- Service provision contracts
- Outsourcing/contracting
- Construct only
- Design and construct (D&C)
- Design, bid, build (DBB)
- Design, construct, maintain (DCM)
- Operate and maintain (O&M)
- Operate, maintain and manage (OM&M)

- Managing contractor
- Alliance contracting

PUBLIC-PRIVATE PARTNERSHIPS VARIANTS

- Build, transfer, operate (BTO)
- Build, operate, transfer (BOT)
- Build, lease, transfer (BLT)
- Build, lease, transfer, maintain (BLTM)
- Build, own, operate, remove (BOOR)
- Build, own, operate, transfer (BOOT)
- Lease, renovate, operate, transfer (LROT)
- Design, build, operate, maintain (DBOM)
- Design, build, finance, operate (DBFO)
- Design, construct, manage, finance (DCMF)
- Design, build, finance, operate, maintain (DBFOM)
- Build, own, operate (BOO)

OTHER APPROACHES

- Lease
- Franchise
- Concession
- Joint venture (JV)
- Regulatory asset base (RAB) model for distinct assets
- Corporatization
- Outright privatization

Source: Grimsey and Lewis (2017).

end of the scale involving design and/or construct, through service provision contracts and outsourcing to, at the other end, outright privatization. On this basis, relationships between the government and the market can be viewed as a continuum. Traditional public funding and provision of services constitute one pole, and purely private activity the other. Partnerships of various types cover most of the points between the two, with each position representing a slightly different mix between the public and private sectors. For example, contracting out could constitute a 'partnership' depending on the precise nature of the responsibilities assigned to the private and public entities under the terms of the contract. Normally, however, PPPs are longer lasting and are more complex due to intricate financing arrangements and the contractual and organizational issues involved.

At the other end of the scale are PPPs as a form of privatization. Savas (2000), we recall, definitely thought so (see p. 21). Moreover, given the degree of ownership rights and responsibilities transferred to the private sector party over an extended period, many other observers also equate PPPs with privatization. A further complication comes from the distinction between brownfield and greenfield projects. Greenfield projects involve the construction and operation of new infrastructure rather than the taking over and refurbishment of existing assets or so-called brownfield projects. This distinction arose early in the literature on PPPs. Consider, for example, the PPP agenda outlined by Michael Gerrard (2001 [2005a]) from Partnerships UK in the IMF's *Finance and Development.*

Gerrard's PPP agenda includes the management of existing public assets as well as the construction of new infrastructure. Previously, PPPs were thought of mainly as vehicles for the provision of new public sector facilities through which services were provided to the public. This change of emphasis underscores the question of whether, and how, PPPs differ from privatization. One reason is that within a PPP contractual relationship the public sector acquires and pays for services from the private sector on behalf of the community and retains the ultimate responsibility for the delivery of the services, although they are being provided by the private sector over an extended period of time (25 years or longer). By contrast when a government entity is privatized, the private firm that takes over the business also takes on the responsibility for service delivery.

Consider, next, the article by Hodgson (1995 [2005a]). Traditional public sector procurement methods have generally resulted in the award of design and/or construct contracts. However, as Hodgson argued, 'the public sector's record in the design and construction of capital schemes is poor. Time and cost overruns are common. Part of the reason lies in the attitudes and culture of the public sector. In the construction sector this often results in conservative or over-engineered designs' (p. 68). Traditional methods also leave the government with a number of risks including that of asset ownership, the risk that the economic value of the asset either during or at the end of the contract term may vary from the value upon which the financial structure of the project is based.

The critical innovation of a design and build contract such as a DBFO or DBFOM road is that it is not a capital asset procurement policy but a service procurement policy. The infrastructure from which the contracted services and, where appropriate, the core services are delivered belongs to the private party which is responsible for the creation of the infrastructure (design and construction risks), the life of the infrastructure (part of the operating risk) and, in many cases, the 'after-life' of the infrastructure (residual value and obsolescence risks).

As Hodgson noted, the DBFO concessionaire will have to assume substantial risk, the intention being that the government body will be buying a road service and not just a new road. Concessionaires will have to be capable of long-term commitment and, as a result, will need to be both robust and committed to quality of performance in this market. To encourage this high quality of service, the structure for the concessions will incorporate a payment system that includes both incentives and penalties. Achieving an appropriate transfer of risk is the primary aim and includes all or some of design risk, construction risk, opening date risk, traffic risk, legislative and force majeure risk, and operational risk. These features, pioneered in the case of road schemes, have now become standard operate-transfer contract.

A feature of many of the PPP contract forms is the commitment of private sector finance to the construction or renovation of the facilities. Underpinning the development of the PPP concept has been an appropriate model for harnessing the supply of private finance for infrastructure projects. This need was achieved by employing project financing techniques pioneered in the 1970s and 1980s in international markets for the financing of energy projects, the key feature being that projects are income-producing and borrowings can be repaid from these proceeds. Future income flows are earmarked for the service of the borrowings, routed through a special purpose vehicle, so divorcing the servicing of the loans from the financial fortunes of the owners or sponsors of the venture.

REASSESSING CONVENTIONAL PROCUREMENT

This chapter has reviewed the factors, and the associated literature, which led to PPPs entering the scene and being employed for infrastructure projects. In many countries, the dominant public sector role in producing, delivering and financing infrastructure services, which held sway for most of the twentieth century, gave way to experimentation with a variety of ways of engaging private sector resources for infrastructure. Part of this regeneration of interest in private sector participation must be seen as a continuation and extension of public sector reforms, which have seen the commercialism of many activities previously regarded as state monopolies. But this was not the only factor.

Much of the revival can be attributed to dissatisfaction with traditional methods of public procurement of infrastructure. Infrastructure policies after World War II had, in the words of the World Bank, been driven by a faith that governments could succeed where markets appeared to fail, but the reality proved to be different. Public sector infrastructure projects in many parts of the world were marked by inefficiency, unreliability and poor fiscal control

(World Bank, 1994). It is easy to overlook now what an important issue this was at the time. The performance of traditional procurement, indifferent at best, led to the growth of DBFO-type arrangements in road construction and to the search for more cooperative 'partnering' approaches in construction projects. These two can be regarded as forerunners of the PPP concept. Both were analyzed in some detail in Grimsey and Lewis (2004b), to which the reader is referred.[2]

A number of studies examined traditional procurement (Flybjerg et al., 2002; Mott MacDonald, 2002) and confirmed the results of earlier research (Fouracre et al., 1990; Pickrell, 1990). Evidence was presented on the extent of cost overruns and revenue shortfalls on infrastructure investments – introducing into the literature on infrastructure procurement phenomena that have come to be known under the headings 'appraisal optimism' and 'optimism bias'.

Various suggestions were made about what to do and how to improve conventional procurement procedures. In particular, Flyvbjerg et al. looked to four basic remedies. The first was increased transparency and public involvement. Second was the use of performance specifications, substituting a goal-driven approach based on outputs in place of the conventional technical-driven procedures that focus on means rather than ends. Third, there was seen to be the need to formulate a clear set of rules governing the project development, construction and operation. The fourth was the inclusion of private risk capital in public infrastructure, so that projects are subject to the market test.

Taking up these points, using a different tack, Darrin Grimsey and I wondered in 2004 whether PPPs might offer one answer, on the grounds that all of the suggested ways of improving public procurement are core elements of a well-structured PPP programme. The PPP agenda focuses on clearly defining outputs, revolves around a detailed business case and project development phase, puts in place project and contract management plans, and involves market testing at a number of levels. A PPP structure also militates against 'ownership' of the appraisal system by one group and should provide for public scrutiny at a number of points. PPPs actually add a fifth element to the four remedies suggested by Flyvbjerg et al., and this is a rigorous and robust competitive tendering process.

These proposals came in the wake of early evidence of PPP performance vis-à-vis traditional procurement. The UK's National Audit Office (NAO) undertakes a rolling review of all government procurement, including Private Financing Initiative (PFI) procurement involving PPPs, and in February 2003 it examined PFI construction performance. An earlier NAO study in 1999 found that only 30 per cent of non-PFI major construction projects were delivered on time and that only 27 per cent were within budget. By comparison, its investigation into PFI construction outcomes showed that the vast majority of PFI projects were constructed on time or early. In contrast to traditionally procured projects, the PFI projects were largely being delivered on time (76 per cent versus 30 per cent) and on budget (78 per cent versus 27 per cent). Moreover, in no case did the public sector bear the cost of construction over-runs, a significant improvement on previous non-PFI conventional procurement experience where the financial costs of projects that ran into difficulties were borne by taxpayers.

While the preliminary evidence did seem to indicate that PPPs offered one solution to the public procurement problem, there is an important sense in which Flyvbjerg et al. were right in having some misgivings about concession-based approaches (they did not canvass partnership arrangements as such). Construction of the asset is only one part of a public–private infrastructure arrangement, and the obligations of the sponsors do not stop at the completion of the facility. Those authors were also correct to highlight that public–private sector contractual agreements place very different, and more testing, demands upon the public sector bodies involved.

In conclusion, as it turned out, this exchange of views and PPP versus conventional procurement performance statistics proved to be only the opening salvos between supporters of PPPs and, what appears to be, at least judged by the reports by Eurodad (2018) and the European Court of Auditors (2018) discussed in Chapter 1, a growing and resolute group opposed to PPPs in any shape or form. Of course, PPPs were never going to replace conventional procurement. They are too big and costly, for starters. Nevertheless, their original unpopularity and continued disfavour today does warrant explanation.

NOTES

1. Four of the seven companies failed to raise capital on the first attempt and were either taken over by other interests or needed financial support from others.
2. Partnering is an idea that originated in the engineering literature, and non-legally binding partnering agreements have been employed in construction projects. Such agreements emphasize developing a 'shared vision' for a project. The aim is to turn away from competition and adversarial relationships, abuse of power, self-interest, lack of trust and dysfunctional markets. Levitt et al. (2019) give a number of illustrations of their use in construction projects across the globe. In Australia, for example, partnering agreements are part of the alliance contracting approach that partnering represents, and these have gained considerable popularity. Such agreements are not needed in PPPs where the formal partnership agreement itself is in operation, and cements in place the project goals, albeit in a more contractual – and not always cooperative – way (Grimsey and Lewis, 2017).

3. Exploring what PPPs can and cannot do

CHARACTERISTICS OF PPPS REVISITED

While some partnerships are created for the purpose of policy formulation, priority setting and coordinating organizations from the various sectors (e.g. crime prevention strategies, educational action), the primary (but not exclusive) concern here is with asset-based services and long-term service provision contracts related to social and economic infrastructure. Typically, such public private partnerships (PPPs) involve a contract, or concession agreement, between a government agency and a single private entity to design, build, finance, operate and/or maintain a facility, usually where the private entity is a special purpose vehicle (SPV) established exclusively for the intended purpose with a number of private firms providing funds or services to the company and putting together a financing package for the SPV that comprises equity from the company's sponsors and debt provided by bonds or commercial loans. The equity and debt are secured solely by the revenue stream that the SPV receives from the operation of the facility.

Some features of the arrangement are as follows:

Focus on services. The emphasis is on services received by government, not government procurement of economic or social infrastructure assets. Government pays for services provided by the private party, which are delivered through privately owned or rented infrastructure as part of the service package.

Relationship. PPPs seek to draw upon the best available skills, knowledge and resources, whether they are in the public or the private sector, and deliver value for money in the provision of public infrastructure services. For this to happen, each partner must transfer resources (money, property, authority, reputation) and specific skills and knowledge to the arrangement.

Whole-of-life-cycle costing. With a PPP contract there is the opportunity for a complete integration – under one party – of upfront design and construction costs with ongoing service delivery, operational, maintenance and refurbishment costs.

Innovation. A PPP approach focuses on output specifications, and provides enhanced opportunities and incentives for bidders to fashion innovative solutions to meet those requirements.

Risk allocation. Risk retained by government in owning and operating infrastructure typically carries substantial, often unvalued, cost. Transferring some of the risk to a private party, which can manage it at less cost, can substantially lower the overall cost to government.

Sharing. PPPs involve a sharing of responsibility and risk for outcomes (whether financial, economic, environmental or social) in a collaborative framework. This mutual responsibility contrasts with relationships between the public and private sectors in which the public body retains control over policy decisions after getting the advice of private sector entities. It also contrasts with relations between the public and private sectors that are primarily contractual in nature and involve essentially command relationships. In these cases, the private sector bodies are not partners in any real sense. There has to be a mutual interest and shared commitment.

Continuity. Partnerships must be enduring and relational. Underpinning the partnership will be a framework contract, which sets out the 'rules of the game' and provides the partners with some certainty. Its existence enables the parties involved to make decisions without having to start from scratch each time and develop from first principles the rules that govern these interactions. While the PPP contract provides the basic architecture of the arrangement, it is necessarily 'incomplete' and does not (and cannot) specify all components and allow for all eventualities. Additionally, there must be shared values, a common understanding of priorities and policy objectives, and a good measure of trust.

The PPP works as follows. The parties commit themselves at the outset to a more cooperative relationship, with the expectation that they will each contribute something of value to the project. The public sector has command over assets such as land, property and the negotiated right of way and brings to the development process the authority to implement the infrastructure acquisition within a planning process. The private sector brings access to outside capital, technical expertise and an incentive structure to develop projects in the most effective manner. As a consequence of the 'discipline' of the private capital markets, there is pressure to improve efficiency in construction and operations, and complete projects at the lowest cost and in the shortest time period. There must then be close control of the operational phase of the facility to ensure security of the cash flows that are needed to repay the project finance. A PPP is all about putting in place appropriate strategies for appraising and managing the risks. Having equity capital and borrowings at risk introduces into the calculation an element of realism that is not possible to obtain when the project is being publicly funded.

Among the key ingredients of such an arrangement are:

- a focus on services, with the emphasis on the delivery of infrastructure services using new or refurbished public infrastructure assets;
- planning and specification, so that government's desired outcomes and output specifications are clear to the market;
- creating a viable business case for the private party;
- certainty of process, ensuring that any conditions to be fulfilled are clearly understood before the project proceeds;
- project resourcing to enable government to advance the project and address issues in line with published time frames;
- clear contractual requirements, centred on key performance specifications, to create incentives that promote performance and minimize disputes;
- formation of a partnership to encourage good faith and goodwill between government and the private party in all project dealings; and
- contract management to monitor and implement the contract.

Rather than there being a 'model' of a partnership, PPPs should be thought of as a process, designed to ensure that all the risks are valued and taken into account in a meaningful way. Because both parties have committed resources and prestige to the success of the project, the partnership relies upon a detailed step-by-step analysis of cost-sharing arrangements, risk mitigation and risk allocation. A PPP is accordingly an incentive-oriented, performance-based arrangement in which contractors are given responsibility for design as well as construction.

At this juncture it is timely to examine the conceptual underpinnings of the PPPs relative to traditional procurement methods.

THE THEORY OF PPPS

What are the characteristics of PPPs that differentiate them from conventional procurement? Three features of a PPP that may cause its productive efficiency to differ from traditional procurement: ownership, bundling and risk transfer (Blanc-Brude et al., 2006).

'Ownership' Rights

According to Blanc-Brude et al. (2006), ownership rights are a good starting point for considering the economic consequences of PPPs, under incomplete contracting arrangements (Macniel, 1974; Grossman and Hart, 1986; Hart and Moore, 1990). Under a PPP, the public sector transfers land, property or facilities controlled by it to the private sector, which is given ownership or control rights for the term of the concession or lease.

Consider a design, build, finance, operate, maintain (DBFOM) contract developed for UK roads. The contractor was responsible for design, construction, maintenance and operation, and also had to finance the project either through its own arrangements or in conjunction with the public entity. But no permanent rights of ownership were conferred on the developer, nor did the developer at any point acquire any interest in the land. Throughout the contract period the Secretary of State remained the highway authority. Instead, the DBFOM contractor was given a right of access to the road, and effectively a 'licence' to operate it, normally for a period of 30 years. Unlike in French-style concessions, this right did not include the collection of user charges. Payment was made on some combination of 'shadow tolls', availability measures and performance indicators (Grimsey and Lewis, 2004b).

Nevertheless, assigning the residual control rights in this way provides an incentive for the private sector entity to undertake relation-specific cost-saving investment (e.g. on road maintenance technology) that increases productive efficiency. In their absence the private firm could not be sure that the investment would pay off and there might be underinvestment in the new technology. Turning over the control rights for the infrastructure can alleviate this problem. However, the act of assignment does not constitute privatization.

Bundling

Another, perhaps the defining, characteristic of a PPP is 'bundling', whereby the construction and operation of the infrastructure is combined in a single contractual framework. This aspect has been explored thoroughly in the literature. Hart (2003) develops a theoretical model to examine the economic efficiency of 'bundling' from an 'incomplete' contracting perspective, in which imperfections arise because it is hard to foresee and contract about uncertain future events. PPPs are generally entered into for a lengthy period of time, usually 20 to 30 years, and are developed in an environment of uncertainty. As such they exhibit, as Hart suggests, the characteristics of 'incomplete' contracts, and their usefulness as integrated arrangements hinges on the nature of contracting costs. His model compares a 'bundled' contract for facility construction and service provision with 'unbundled' conventional public procurement in which the government first contracts with a builder to construct the facility and then later contracts with another private sector party to operate and run the facility. The choice between the two alternatives, bundled versus unbundled, turns on whether it is easier to write contracts on service provision than on building provision.

Hart's model leads to a straightforward result. Under the assumed conditions, conventional provision ('unbundling') is better if the quality of the building can be clearly specified whereas the quality of the service cannot. Contrariwise, the PPP is better if the quality of the service can be well specified in the initial contract (or, more generally, there are good performance indicators that can be used to reward or penalize the service provider) whereas the quality of the building cannot. Hart surmises that schools may fall into the first category. Contracting on the building is relatively simple, while contracting on the service may not be. On the other hand, hospitals may fall into the second category in that although specifying service quality is far from straightforward, it may be easier to come up with reasonable performance measures concerning how patients are treated than it is to specify what is likely to be a very complex building (ibid., C73–4).

Bundling is also advanced on the grounds of enhancing the potential to realize economies of scale and scope along with innovations in design, pricing and risk sharing. Usually, however, the build, operate, transfer (BOT) concessionaires are joint ventures of a number of private companies which agree in advance to subcontract each of the different activities and take equity stakes in the SPV to cement the relationship. Two problems may thereby be introduced. First, good constructors may be teamed with not so good financiers. Second, competition is limited to those bodies which are part of the group. Companies with good technical know-how but poor financial capability may be unable to bid because the activities are jointly, rather than separately, auctioned.

For these reasons, Trujillo et al. (1998) examine the case for unbundling. They recognize that the costs of unbundling (e.g. creating different entities, monitoring the specifications in the different stages, and achieving interface) may be considerable, but may be offset by an improved allocation of risk. On the other hand, it must be conceded that 'unbundling' is effectively what happens already under a PPP since the concessionaire rarely assumes all the project risks and many of the risks are put out to a range of specialist contractors.[1] There is, nevertheless, an important difference between the two situations. Incentives are stronger when the supplier is bearing at least some of the risks of supply. The assumption of overall responsibility prior to risk transfer gives the concession winner the appropriate incentives to do the job properly, which may not be present to the same degree when there is a nexus between the principal (the public body) and the agent (the private sector service company coordinating entity).[2] Also, a feature of PPPs is that risks are usually shared between the private sector and the public sector, with the government 'taking back' some risks for which private bodies would charge 'too much'. For this risk allocation process to be implemented, the government might find it less costly to negotiate with a single body rather than with a host of individual subcontractors, either directly or by proxy through the coordinating company.

Daniels and Trebilcock (1996) consider that the case for bundling and vertical integration is much the same as that for the existence of firms in economic theory, and rests on the presence not only of contracting costs (examined by Hart), but also information costs and economies of scale and scope.[3] In effect, the case for integrating design, construction, finance, operations and maintenance is that private firms can coordinate these activities at lower cost than can government, and they are better able to respond to economic incentives.

The position that Darrin Grimsey and I have articulated in our writings is that the question of incentives is central. In real estate, the old mantra is location, location, location. In economics, the appropriate mantra is incentives, incentives, incentives. It is the welding of upfront design and financial engineering to downstream management of the construction costs and revenue flow that gives the PPP its distinctive incentive compatibility characteristics. As one example, financiers also have incentives to make sure that services are supplied on time and to the requisite standard when the revenue stream that is generated represents the main source for repaying debt. In addition, bundling allows for the internalization of externalities between the construction and operation phases of the project (Blanc-Brude et al., 2006). Integrating construction and operations offers an incentive to make larger upfront outlays in the construction phase in order to achieve lower life-cycle maintenance costs. In the absence of bundling, these externalities would not be taken into account by the contractor, and productive efficiency would be lower.[4]

Risk Transfer

The transfer of risk to the private sector can also render a PPP more cost-efficient than traditional procurement. Grout (1997, 2003, 2005) emphasizes information costs and the incentive structure created by the PPP service payment mechanism. Determining responsibility for cost overruns is a serious source of conflict when there are design changes or other unexpected developments. Writing the contract in terms of the flow of services from the infrastructure facility rather than the process of construction can significantly change the incentive system. If, for example, the contractor is responsible for both construction and supplying the services but is remunerated only for the successful provision of services of a suitable quality, the entity needs to build the correct facility, get the delivery process right, and contain costs while not sacrificing quality. These incentives can be blunted under traditional procurement if, by virtue of the contract, the public sector carries most of the risk of construction cost and delays.

Indeed, in all respects, an effective transfer of risk from the public to the private sector can lead to a more explicit treatment of risk, since it is the acceptance of risk that gives the private entity the motivation to price and produce efficiently. Private finance (debt and equity) is potentially important to this process, although its role has been overlooked in the theoretical PPP literature. Private finance incorporates an assessment of project risk. Under government financing, the cost of capital is artificially low, because the public sector can transfer risks to taxpayers and end-users without having to compensate them. This under-pricing of risk in traditional procurement skews decision-making by removing it from the incentives to prevent cost overruns and project delays that would put revenue streams needed to repay debt under threat.

These insights carry implications for the *ex ante* costs of constructing infrastructure under a PPP in comparison with traditional procurement. Asset construction costs should be higher under a PPP whenever there is scope for relation-specific, cost-saving investments to be made. Likewise, construction costs under bundled contracts will exceed those with unbundling if there is the potential to make additional outlays in the construction phase which lead to life-cycle cost savings. Construction costs will also be higher under PPPs because of the explicit recognition, quantification and pricing of construction and other risks transferred to the private sector partner, who will want to be compensated for carrying them. In general terms, this would appear to be the case based on a study of European road projects, with the largest part of the estimated difference seemingly representing the cost of passing on construction risk to the private entity (Blanc-Brude et al., 2006). In effect, it would seem that the public sector pays more, say, for a PPP road *ex ante* primarily to avoid time and cost overruns. Since changes due to client requirements are the main cause of cost variations in both PPP and traditionally procured projects, 'one of the arguments for PPP is that the process of preparing detailed output based specifications makes the public sector focus on exactly what it wants. Hence changes causing cost increases become less likely. Besides, the incentive to present realistic construction budgets are weaker in traditional procurement, given weaker accountability in the event of cost overruns' (ibid. p. 32). Overall, the authors conclude that 'while it would thus seem that the transfer of the construction risk is successful in PPPs' one cannot nevertheless conclude that it unambiguously creates 'value for money', because 'the public sector could transfer construction risk in traditional public procurement by entering fixed-price, date-certain construction contracts' and 'making use of schemes to provide incentives' (ibid., p. 31). On this basis, the efficiency case for risk transfer under a PPP is suggestive, but certainly not conclusive.

MYTHS AND MISCONCEPTIONS ABOUT PPPS

In this section we review the seven 'myths' about the costs and benefits of PPP as set out by Monk et al. (2019). This is followed by the analysis of 'misconceptions' by Engel et al. (2014).

Myths

Myth 1: PPPs provide new private funds to pay for public infrastructure

In whatever way the infrastructure is financed, the investment cost and operating costs must ultimately be repaid from taxes assessed on citizens at various levels, from tolls or other user fees paid for by the users of the asset, or from some combination of these two sources. PPPs have often been presented as a way to fund infrastructure without imposing new taxes on the public. The authors (Monk et al.) accept that it is factually accurate to state that a PPP which will be entirely paid for by user fees does not require new taxes to be levied, but this is misleading. They argue that, on opportunity cost grounds,

> users will now have to pay new or higher tolls or other usage fees for an asset that might otherwise have been fully or partly paid for by taxes, and then provided to users free or with lower, more subsidized user fees: lower tolls in the case of a highway or bridge, and free or lower passenger fares in the case of a transit project. (Monk et al., 2019, p. 33)

Myth 2: Public financing in the United States is less costly than private financing

The argument here relates to the special case of the use of tax-exempt bonds in the United States, and is of little interest outside of those shores, except for the general point commonly made that the reduced cost of public tax-exempt bond financing for a specific infrastructure project must be more than offset by a combination of risk transfer and other public benefits to make PPP delivery with private financing a preferred alternative to traditional public delivery with tax-exempt (i.e. cheaper) public financing.

Myth 3: The only benefit of a PPP is privately arranged financing

While it is the case that private financing can help to augment or replace government financing, the authors argue that it delivers five additional benefits:

1. PPPs can dramatically increase the available sources of financing to build needed infrastructure.
2. Transferring some or all of the project risks to the PPP concessionaire protects the state from mishaps and cost overruns. This, in turn, creates

a level of profit-driven discipline that is often lacking in publicly funded projects.

3.   Under life-cycle costing, decisions tend to focus on optimizing life-cycle sustainability rather than simply on minimizing first cost or operating cost.
4.   Innovative construction methods can reduce design and construction time by up to two years when compared to a traditional design, bid, build public procurement approach. This time saving can help offset the higher cost of PPP financing.
5.   PPPs guarantee maintenance. Often, when public finances are under pressure, the first thing to be cut is the maintenance of existing infrastructure assets, increasing costs down the line. PPP contracts, by contrast, typically impose stringent performance standards for maintenance which, if not met, impose financial penalties on the concessionaire. Thus assets tend to be reliably well maintained.

Myth 4: PPPs mean imposing tolls, and voters dislike tolls
This is almost a truism, certainly not confined as the authors imply to the East Coast of the United States. It is very difficult to change matters once 'free' freeways are introduced.

Myth 5: PPPs represent a new and untested infrastructure procurement policy in the United States
Not so; in fact, the private sector has been a partner in various US infrastructure projects for more than 200 years – witness the canals and the turnpikes beginning with the Virginia Act of 1785. By the 1840s nearly 1600 turnpike companies had been chartered, along with private toll bridges. In the 1900s they were acquired as the states established their highway systems.

Myth 6: PPPs are the same as privatizations
This issue was dealt with in Chapter 2.

Myth 7: The private sector's profit in PPPs comes at the expense of the public sector
A PPP harnesses the private sector in the areas where it can provide additional value for money. Thus, the objective is to find situations where the private sector can manage to create sufficient profit, while still adding net value for the public sector by aligning interests and allocating risks to the people best able to manage them. Monk et al. consider that this can be done in a variety of ways, such as through accelerated project delivery. Project planners can also define risks that are optimally shouldered by the private sector, and those that should remain with the public sector. Any government's choice in this respect should

rest on its ability to find value for money from the public project that does not come at the expense of the public sector.

Misconceptions

Advocates of PPPs advance a number of arguments to suggest that PPPs can assist governments to provide infrastructure services more efficaciously. Engel et al. (2014) summarize the possible reasons under six headings, to which is added here a seventh, and their framework is used to evaluate what PPPs can do, and what they cannot.

Misconception 1: PPPs bring in additional finance

With government budgets under strain, and a considerable infrastructure gap to fill, it is often argued that private finance is needed to take up the slack. Revenues to the private sector firm can come from two sources: customer payments or public sector payments (or some combination thereof). If the customer revenue sources are tolls, user charges (i.e. from a sporting facility) or value capture, then private finance does indeed add additional resources for infrastructure, since the user payments, say, enable the private body to repay the finance it has raised. Equally, of course, the government could have raised the capital itself and used the customer revenue collected to fund (i.e. repay) its borrowings.

On the other hand, when the source of revenue to the PPP SPV comprises payments from the public sector party, the government is effectively funding the project and repaying the private finance over time via the unitary charge. No additional non-government resources for infrastructure are tapped over the long haul. The PPP does not bring in extra funds. Instead, the PPP alters the timing of financing and funding flows, enabling the provision of public infra-structure services to be brought forward. It is analogous to leasing a car and enjoying motoring services rather than buying the car and paying for it in full up front. In this case, the infrastructure is built by a private consortium using its own (or financiers') money and, in effect, leased back to the government for a fee before the public eventually takes full ownership at the end of the contract.

Misconception 2: Private sector efficiency

If we start from the premise (to which not everyone would ascribe) that private sector firms are more efficient than public enterprises, then the injection of private sector enterprise and innovation into infrastructure projects via the PPP arrangement might be expected to produce efficiency gains. However, this result is not obviously the case, unless we are comparing the PPP with tradi-tional government-built public works. For the most part, public procurement nowadays is left to private contractors who are hired by the government under various separate, individual contracts to design, build, operate and maintain the infrastructure assets. Furthermore, invariably the private contractors wear two hats, because many of the firms doing so are the very same ones which also bid for PPP contracts and are responsible for the provision of infrastructure services under these arrangements.

Presumably, any efficiency gains must stem from what differs between the two alternatives, specifically 'bundling'. Bundling allows the private entity to influence every part of the project and respond to the very different incentive structure that a PPP arrangement embodies, as already discussed.

Nonetheless, in terms of realizing efficiency gains, PPPs face a further hurdle. Where a PPP requires the private party to raise finance, the efficiency gains need to be large enough to overcome the higher cost of private finance vis-à-vis government capital raising. Whether the cost of capital for the public sector is really lower than that for the private sector or merely reflects that the public sector does not default because it can levy taxes to repay debt is an 'old saw', dating back to Vickrey (1964), Solow (1965) and Arrow and Lind (1970). On one side, there is the view that the public sector can better absorb and spread risks among many individuals. On the other side, the opposing view is that government imposes a contingent liability upon taxpayers for which they are not renumerated, and that this cost should be built into government borrowing costs. If this were done, the real cost of government borrowing would be the same as the private sector if the underlying risks of the projects are identical. Lind (1982) observed that 'the profession is no closer to agreement on the theory, on a procedure for computing the discount rate, or on the rate itself than it was in 1966', and this remains true today.

Misconception 3: Regulation through competition
A considerable literature exists on the optimal pricing of public services (e.g. 'classics' on public utility pricing, peak-load pricing, telephone service charges and electricity tariffs are collected together in Turvey, 1968). At a practical level, however, prices charged by public utilities may, because of political pressures, be set too low, encouraging overconsumption and underinvestment. Or, they may be too high due to over-staffing, bureaucratic procedures and inefficient operations. These problems do not disappear when the entity is privatized. Prices may be too high because the privatized firm has a natural monopoly. Even if regulated, excessive profits or 'satisficing' behaviour (Cyert and March, 1963) or over-investment (which has to be recovered from higher charges) may result from regulatory capture. Alternatively, political pressure may be brought upon the regulatory agency to keep user fees low, although the potential for the cost-of-services approach to be 'gamed' due to asymmetric information makes this outcome less likely.

Engel et al. (2014, p. 17) contend that PPPs at least offer the promise of being closer to efficient pricing for two reasons. First, in their operation, they do not depend on government and are somewhat insulated from political influences due to their explicit contractual relationship. Second, PPPs may introduce a competitive process for determining prices in place of the setting of rates by what they call an 'imperfect regulator'. Like contracting out arrangements, the private party running the PPP is chosen by means of a competitive auction in which the principal bidding variable is the user fee or charge. Competition, but for the market as opposed to competition in it, can lead in these circumstances to efficient pricing by eliminating economic rents accruing to the service provider.

Misconception 4: Better road pricing
Fourth, in the case of public roads, it is widely accepted that tolls and charges paid by most road users, but especially trucking and haulage operators, do not cover wear and tear or the costs of maintaining the road system, requiring governments to draw upon general revenue to do so. PPP toll roads can help to address this imbalance. They can also lead the way to congestion and other pricing regimes.

Misconception 5: Avoiding 'white elephants'
Fifth, the large amount of infrastructure that would qualify for the description 'white elephants' suggests the need for procedures that filter out projects that are over-engineered, or do not warrant being constructed. PPPs may serve this purpose if they are funded by user charges, since financiers presumably will not wish to finance such projects, nor will the projects attract equity capital. It is difficult to ascertain exactly how many bad projects did not pass such a market test and were judged to be 'un-bankable'. What we do know for sure, however, is that still too many have slipped through the net.

Misconception 6: Public interest issues
Sixth, it is not hard to find that there are many individuals and welfare groups who object to PPP toll roads because they are unfair to low-income users, who cannot afford to pay the tolls regularly. If we dismiss the view (increasingly widespread) that all roads and all public services should be 'free', and that it is the rich who should pay for them, a number of points can be made in favour of user-pay PPP highways. First, if users use the toll roads, traffic will be freed up on free public roads (which often follow much the same route as the motorways). Second, toll roads provide the option to pay for speed of movement. Third, since tolls fund the road infrastructure, the burden on general taxes is lowered. Note, as an aside, it is the case that low-income households generally pay little income tax. In Australia, 48 per cent of the 12.2 million

'income units' pay no net tax. Any tax they do contribute is more than offset by welfare – pensions, family tax benefits or childcare rebates – that they receive, making them net recipients from government (National Centre for Social and Economic Modelling, 2014).

Misconception 7: PPPs are one-offs

Seventh, PPPs are commonly seen as idiosyncratic, one-off projects. This viewpoint is misguided for two reasons. One is that it ignores international experience. When Australia introduced PPPs, it adopted a 'bespoke' commercial principles approach that eschewed developing standard form contracts for PPPs (Gleeson et al., 2019). This was in stark contrast to the UK and Canada that both developed standard contracts. Australian PPPs have been criticized for how costly they are to set up and for the private sector to bid on. They also tended to be led by legal considerations when framing the contract. This resulted in the model tending to be used for the most complex and large projects that could afford the investment costs. The legalistic approach created bespoke contracts that are often difficult to navigate and reinvented the wheel on many issues, albeit in slightly different ways and with slightly different risk allocations.

In contrast, the Canadian PPP model chose to adopt standard risk allocations and, in some cases, standard specifications (e.g. in hospitals) that, while perhaps compromising on idiosyncratic features of projects, have created economies of scale. This enabled the model to be used cost-effectively on smaller and more standard projects. It also relegated the legal side to a secondary role and allowed the parties to focus more attention on technical solutions, that is, design. Given that PPPs are all about service delivery, this seems to be a more satisfactory result.

PPP CONTROVERSIES

Refinancing Opportunities

Relatively early on, in a number of well-publicized cases, SPV debt has been refinanced, boosting the sponsors' rate of return (in one case from 12.8 to 39 per cent p.a., and in another from 19 to 60 per cent p.a.) and providing investment banks with large upfront fees. In one case (Fazakerley prison in the UK), the consortium was able to refinance the project because of its success in delivering the project ahead of time and establishing a track record of operations, lowering the perceived risk of debt. HM Prison Service argued the importance of not removing the opportunities for the private firms to benefit substantially from successful risk-taking. The solution that emerged was a cost-sharing formula to apply to such windfall gains in new contracts, although it remained an issue with existing contracts (House of Commons Committee of Public Accounts, 2006). Revenue-sharing provisions are common for PPP road projects in Australia, with the public sector sharing in toll revenue in excess of base-case forecasts (Brown, 2005).

Drag on Government Budgets

Payments under PPP schemes involve significant fixed payments to cover interest charges and capital repayment. These debt repayment charges introduced into the finances of public sector authorities, such as the British National Health Service trusts, are said to limit the later flexibility of these bodies, by 'mortgaging the future' in return for immediate gains since payments are transferred to the future. The counter-argument is that construction can be brought forward with the cost of infrastructure investment spread over the life of the asset, much as homebuyers do when they take out a home mortgage loan or use leasing and hire purchase facilities. At another level, the contractually binding commitment over the project life for the services included in the project can be criticized for reducing the autonomy of public sector management in relation to discretionary spending. Concurrently, however, it removes the ability to divert funding from needed maintenance work.

Incomplete Risk Transfer

Critics often suggest that there is no substantive risk transfer under a PPP. However, this charge would appear to be truer of the traditional procurement approach of design and construct. Since the builder is not responsible for how the buildings function, there is an implicit temptation to build (or at least tender) cheaply. There is also not an incentive to take into account the whole-of-life trade-offs that might exist. Under a PPP approach the contractor is forced to think longer term and also cannot just 'walk away' having completed the construction. Under the contract, the contractor has ongoing, long-term responsibility for the facility's performance, which is reflected in performance-based monthly payments. Even if the contractor is unable to fulfil its obligations, and terminates the partnership, it cannot take the facility away and, in most cases, the assets revert to the public sector.

Community Access

Concerns are also expressed about community access and user fees charged for access, although these can be addressed in the contract to ensure that access rights are the same as other facilities and that increases in user charges are limited to the rate of inflation or some other predetermined rate. Privately owned and operated toll roads have been especially controversial in Australia. Some, such as Tony Harris (2006, p. 1), are opposed to the very idea: 'in an urban environment toll roads are ridiculous and privately owned toll roads are even more ridiculous'. The objection is that the toll roads break up a complex network into segments with separate tolling creating additional transactions costs (Harris, 1998, p. 6). Another objection raised is that, due to some motorists' aversion to charging, 'direct tolling forces between 20 and 40 per cent of motorists off these low-cost infrastructure facilities on to more expensive stop–start arterial roads and therefore reduces the economic benefits of the facility' (Cox, 2005, p. 8). These difficulties can be avoided by remunerating the contractor through shadow tolls based on availability and other performance indicators (such as surface conditions, lighting and verge conditions). But then other problems arise. Clarke and Hawkins (2006) criticize Melbourne City Link and other urban road networks because the tolls are for cost recovery and are not efficiency-based, such as being higher at peak periods to reflect higher congestion costs. There are no easy answers to such matters. These issues are also being played out in the United States as roads, bridges and airports are being sold off to private interests such as Transurban and Macquarie Infrastructure Group (Thornton, 2007).

Lack of Flexibility

PPP contracts contain detailed specification of the outputs required and the penalties for not meeting them under long-term contracts that typically lack flexibility. If the government wishes to alter its service requirements, this is possible but may prove to be costly. While PPPs in particular have been criticized on this score, the reality is that inflexibility is present regardless of the procurement route. There are few things more irreversible than a building or piece of infrastructure. If flexibility and catering for changing needs is important, then these features need to be incorporated into what is being procured irrespective of the method of procurement. Indeed, PPPs might be said to have merits. First, the PPP model forces upfront consideration of what long-term flexibility is likely to be required to respond to demographic and other changes. Boundaries for flexibility can then be specified and the risk of designing in and delivering on this flexibility can be transferred to the private sector under the PPP. Second, the costs of doing away with all or part of a PPP are accurately known, whereas the costs of changing conventionally procured facilities are hidden from view and are frequently under-costed because such long-run considerations are usually ignored.

Procurement Cost

The average procurement time for PPP projects has been around 22 months in the UK and 12–18 months in Australia. It takes a long time to agree the risk transfers, payments and terms that are acceptable to both parties – imposing considerable legal and due diligence costs on both the contractors and public sector side. The combination of time and due diligence means that multi-million dollar bid costs are at risk. Private parties will expect the contractual arrangements to cover the financial risks that they face. PPPs are generally not recommended for small individual projects, although combining a number of small projects helps to spread procurement costs across several projects. Overall procurement costs could be reduced if it were accepted that PPPs had been sufficiently 'road-tested' in certain applications, thereby dispensing with the (not inconsiderable) cost of preparing the Public Sector Comparator (PSC) against which a PPP bid is compared. A competitive bidding process would then ensure value. This is effectively what France has done with concessions for water and many other municipal services, but such an approach has made only limited headway in other PPP markets.

THE COMPLEXITY OF PPPS

Scott et al. (2019), in the introductory chapter to the book *Public–Private Partnerships for Infrastructure Development* edited by them (Levitt et al., 2019), argue that PPP projects are invariably complex, and that this feature poses distinctive governance challenges. Complexity, they argue, especially on transportation projects, comes from a combination of factors: PPPs embrace multiple tasks, and are uncertain, idiosyncratic, long-lived, multi-phased, expensive transactions involving a large and shifting number of internal and external stakeholders operating within ever-changing contexts. They then go on to elucidate ('unpack') these elements as follows:

1. Project complexity commences with the number and types of tasks that must be performed to accomplish the objective. Campbell (1988, p. 43) proposes that 'any objective task characteristic that implies an increase in information load, information diversity, or rate of information change can be considered a contributor to complexity'. Complexity is increased by the presence of (i) multiple desired goals, (ii) diverse potential ways or paths to arrive at the objective, (iii) conflicting interdependence among paths, and (iv) uncertain links among paths and outcomes (Campbell, 1988).
2. Technical uncertainty relates primarily to the inexact or unknown means–end connection linking activities to their consequences (March and

Simon, 1958). That is, projects vary in the extent to which the technologies are routine, familiar and time-tested or are more experimental and variable in their outcomes. The use of experimental or untested technical processes is not common on transportation projects but may occur on selected components such as bridges or tunnels. Uncertainty is far more likely to be associated with some aspects of the project organization, such as stakeholder composition and/or behaviour, and the project's context, such as uncertain political and institutional conditions.

3. PPP projects are idiosyncratic in the sense that most project organizations are constructed *de novo* for the purpose of constructing a particular link in the transportation system, for example a road from point A to point B. The developers, or some other agency with the proper authority, selects a lead company which then creates an SPV that serves as the focal organization of a unique network of participating organizations, including the public sponsor, financial backers, contractors, operators, clients, regulators and affected parties such as users and the broader public. Scott et al. (2019) consider that, due to the fact that each project begins anew, often with different combinations of participants, projects are 'learning light', unable to carry forward the 'lessons learned' from one project to the next. On this basis, they argue that this is one reason why the existence of broader 'enabling' support structures at the state or regional level are often important to the success of PPPs.

4. Infrastructure projects are relatively long-lived, their development and construction period typically extending over several years and their operation and maintenance over several decades. Because of their associated complexity and uncertainty, Miller and Olleros (2000) argue that the more successful projects are preceded by a long 'shaping' period. Even if the technical problems are modest and the outcomes sought are known, it is important for the SPV participants to consider possible future problems, including how to set up governance arrangements to ensure flexibility among team members.

5. Of necessity, projects are multi-phased, passing from a period of exploration and project conception through to project financing and shaping, followed by a combined period of design and construction, leading into the time of maintenance and operation. These phases draw on different talents and activities, so that any project involves a changing collection of stakeholders as it proceeds from earlier to later stages. The coming and going of a varied set of participants also entails changes over time in the relative significance of project participants. Severe challenges are posed to project governance when, for example, earlier participants make binding decisions that negatively affect later, not yet represented, parties.

6. Scott et al. next consider financing, and the challenges posed by the swings in international finance markets, the global financial crisis, and the more recent aim of tapping institutional investors (e.g. pension funds and sovereign wealth funds) that control 'patient capital' which would seem to be ideal for investing in long-term infrastructure projects. However, the terms 'financing' and 'funding' of infrastructure are often confused. Financing refers to the supply of capital (private or public) used to pay for the upfront investment costs of an infrastructure project. Eventually, however, money is required to repay (and pay a return on) the financing instruments. Funding is then called for, and relates to the revenue sources and income streams used to pay for the costs of the infrastructure over its life. Possible sources of funding are direct user charges (such as road tolls, licence fees, port charges or water charges), value capture from charges on other beneficiaries, or general taxation (Grimsey and Lewis, 2017, p. 24).

7. PPPs rely on a wide and changing group of participants/stakeholders. Balancing their interests greatly adds to the complexity of PPPs. Scott et al. define stakeholders to include all of those who are involved in and affected by the organization and operation of the project group, and they are likely to be a very large and diverse collection. They range from 'internal' stakeholders, for example financiers, stockholders, managers, other employees and contractual partners, to 'external' stakeholders, including 'all of those groups and individuals that can affect, or are affected by, the accomplishment of [the firm's] organizational purpose'(Freeman, 1984, p. 25). Included would be such bodies as the project's exchange partners, government regulators, consumers, affected communities and interested associations.

8. What is perhaps unusual is the extent to which the types of stakeholders associated with a project shift over time. Some, such as developers, are heavily engaged during early phases and are highly influential, but their centrality wanes over time. Later stakeholders, such as project operators, user groups and various civic movements, become much more active and involved over time. The diverse and shifting nature of the stakeholders makes for complex governance arrangements.

If these issues were not enough, Scott et al. finally drew attention to many other factors that complicate the picture. Projects are susceptible to earthquakes, fires, floods, storms, unexpected geological conditions etc. Economic conditions and political considerations impinge, the latter if only because one of the core parties is a government entity. Also singled out are social and institutional risks, legal and regulatory provisions, occupational health and safety matters, and professional standards governing the work of lawyers, engineers and accountants. All of these must mesh together if the project is to succeed.

CONCLUDING REMARKS

In this chapter it has been argued that PPPs are a way of introducing very different incentive structures into the procurement process. The theory of PPPs suggests that incentives to productive efficiencies can be introduced into infrastructure procurement by vesting control rights with the private sector, bundling into one contract the design, construction, operation and maintenance of the facility, and by transferring the risk of cost and time overruns to the private partner. To these arguments there should be added, at a practical level, the disciplines injected by the participation of private capital that is genuinely 'at risk' and that is not priced artificially low and divorced from project risk.

Nonetheless, the literature on PPPs is littered with a number of myths and misconceptions about what they can and cannot achieve, and these have needed to be sorted out. Also, PPPs themselves are not without difficulties. They are too complicated, and costly, for many small projects. Even for larger projects, their complexity presents opportunities for them to be 'gamed' by some participants without a long-term commitment to the project, especially if poorly conceived and designed by the procuring agency. Compounding this behaviour, in some cases, PPP contractual arrangements may be beyond the capacity of the public sector agency to implement and manage. For other projects the tight specification of the outputs required may be difficult to detail for an extended period, leading to the charge that the contracts are too inflexible and consequently hostages to the future. In the next chapter, the idea that PPPs can never be good value is examined.

NOTES

1. In this way, the operation of PPPs can be seen as paralleling the growth of networking and 'virtual corporations' formed by creating groups of contracting partners and taking advantage of digital technology.
2. In general, the separation between principal and agent gives rise to problems of asymmetric information and hidden actions. Effectively, the principal does not know how good the agent is, and cannot easily observe the agent's actions. Sappington (1991) provides a survey.
3. See, for example, Oliver Williamson (1996) and Mark Casson (2000, chapter 5) for analyses of the role of transactions costs and information costs. Economies of scale and scope are examined by Alfred Chandler (1990), as is indicated by his title *Scale and Scope.*
4. As was noted in Chapter 1, there are some similarities between the 'unbundling' issue and the decision of whether to employ a builder for home construction or subcontract oneself the functions of the various trades.

4. Can PPPs ever be good value?

COST OF FINANCE

In Chapter 1 attention was drawn to the dramatic winding back of the UK's Private Finance Initiative (PFI) with the portent that event held for the future role of public private partnerships (PPPs) in infrastructure investment. The PFI had pioneered the use of PPPs, not only in Britain, but globally. As of 2018 only two large privately financed projects were on the books of the UK government, and no new schemes had been brought forward for 18 months. The UK Treasury stated that the existing private partnership model was 'inflexible and overly complex', as reported by The Guardian (2018a) under the heading 'Bye-Bye, PFI: UK Signals Effective End of Private Finance Initiative'. It was further reported that 'PFI fell into disuse because it got difficult to prove that private funding provided better value for money than public funding' (ibid., p. 2). That was at a time when worldwide interest rates were low. Since then, as the COVID-19 recession took hold in 2020, interest rates have fallen even lower, accentuating matters further.

Cost of finance becomes an issue when the private sector raising and supply of finance (usually project finance) is included in the PPP bundle. A recurring question, raised from the very outset, has been: can PPPs ever be good value for money when the government is able to borrow funds from the markets much more cheaply than the private sector can? When the so-called 'PPP premium', namely the extra cost of private sector financing relative to government borrowing, is likely to be 200–300 basis points (2 to 3 percentage points) over a large number of years, it creates a significant hurdle for the PPP project to overcome. On this basis it is contended by the practitioner-based finance publication *Euromoney*, for example, that:

> The other solution (to highway finance) is to finance the project wholly in the public sector, either with government or multilateral funds. It is, after all, more expensive to raise debt on a project finance basis. When considered alongside the guarantees and commitments which have to be provided to attract commercial finance, the best approach would be to borrow on a sovereign basis.[1]

Others, while conceding the existence of the PPP premium, nevertheless accept that PPPs can surmount the differential financing hurdle and still offer value for money because the private sector is able to deliver sufficient cost savings in other aspects of the project (design, construction, operation, management).

Grimsey and Lewis (2004b) drew attention to the fact that a number of writers consider that the 'lower government borrowing cost' argument is seriously flawed (especially Kay, 1993; Grout, 1997; Klein, 1997; and Argy et al., 1999). Both Grout and Klein adopt a position that in some ways is similar to the famous Modigliani–Miller theorem about the cost of capital. Modigliani and Miller argued that the 'true' value of a firm is governed by the risk characteristics of the underlying stream of returns, and (in the no tax regime case) is independent of how finance is raised. Analogously, Grout as well as Klein argue that what is important is the 'true' risk of the project, which is independent of whether the public sector or the private sector provides the finance. What differs is that the private provision of finance in the PPP route explicitly builds risk into the cost of funds, whereas traditional public procurement masks the risk because the government can finance the project at a risk-free interest rate independent of the actual risk position. As John Kay has remarked: 'we would lend to the government even if we thought it would burn the money or fire it off into space' (1993, p. 63).

But why can government borrow at a risk-free rate of interest? This reflects the fact that (and again we quote John Kay) 'the cost of debt both to governments and to private firms is influenced predominately by the perceived risk of default rather than an assessment of the quality of returns from the specific investment' (ibid., p. 63). For private debt there is a risk of default. For government debt, there is little or none (at least in the case of governments of most advanced countries). The traditional answer to the question of why the government borrows at a risk-free rate is provided by Arrow and Lind (1970): that the public sector can better absorb and spread risks among a greater number of individuals (see also Moszoro, 2016). Arrow and Lind contend that, under certain conditions, the social cost of bearing the risk of a given public sector project approaches zero as the risk is spread over an increasing number of taxpayers, with both individual and aggregate risk premiums falling to zero as the number of taxpayers becomes infinitely large. Notably, their conclusion is driven not by greater diversification or pooling of public investment projects (as argued by Samuelson (1964) and Vickrey (1964) for example) but by the large number of taxpayers over which project risk can be distributed. A key passage in their analysis states that:

> ... when the risks associated with a public investment are publicly borne, the total cost of risk-bearing is insignificant and, therefore, the government should ignore uncertainty in evaluating public investments ... This result is obtained not because the government is able to pool investments but because the government distributes the risk associated with any investment among a large number of people. It is the

risk-spreading aspect of government investment that is essential to this result. (Arrow and Lind, 1970, p. 366)

In effect, the government is risk-free in the eyes of an investor lending funds to it, not because of any superior risk pooling ability, but because the risk is transferred to the taxpayers, who bear the cost through the risk of higher future tax payments and different consumption outcomes. In Klein's words, taxpayers have assumed a contingent liability for which they are not remunerated. Essentially, they have become shadow equity providers. This residual risk imposed upon taxpayers is a cost, which ought to enter into any cost–benefit analysis. If this were done, the real cost of government borrowing would be the same as the private sector, if the underlying risk of the projects were the same.

Reductio ad absurdum is a form of argument used by economists when confronted by auditors or accountants or those who can only see the raw numbers before them. Taken to its limit, the lower government borrowing cost argument would seem to imply that all activities should be undertaken or financed by government, since its cost of capital is so low. If only infrastructure is regarded as important enough to so benefit, why not have telecommunications companies, power companies, water suppliers, gas producers, transport companies, steel firms and so on, and all their users and consumers, enjoy the benefits of less expensive infrastructure services due to cheaper finance? This was the situation in the early post-war years, and look where state ownership and control got us. Perhaps more to the point, suppose that the scenario sketched out were to happen but in the different environment of fluid capital and internationally open financial markets without extensive exchange controls; would the government debt still be regarded as riskless by the overseas and other investors?

Obviously, public debt is not riskless. For central government debt there is the risk that debt can be 'monetized' (by printing money), while at the regional level of government there is the risk of adverse economic performance. Nevertheless, in comparison with private bodies, governments enjoy near risk-free status because they can resort to general taxes and 'inflation' taxation (i.e. inflating the debt away by reducing its real purchasing power) to avoid bankruptcy. Private firms and individuals are, by contrast, exposed to this 'taxation risk', an externality ignored in risk evaluation but which needs to be built into social risk calculations.

The corollary is that the higher credit rating of governments, and hence their lower borrowing rates, is largely irrelevant to the choice between public and private provision of infrastructure. Grimsey and Lewis (2004b) noted the position of Argy et al. (1999) who argued that, subject to three conditions, the cost of capital should be assumed to be the same for both the public and private sectors. These conditions are:

1. that the risks associated with the specific project (variance in returns) are mainly 'commercial' rather than policy-related in character;
2. that the private capital market is reasonably efficient; and
3. that private sector financing transaction costs (being on a smaller scale) are not overwhelmingly large relative to those usually incurred by the public sector.

According to those authors, these three conditions probably do hold for many new infrastructure projects so that, provided the rewards match the risk, reliance upon the private sector for provision should not entail any extra capital cost (and, indeed, if the private sector is more efficient at project design and managing the capital, the capital cost could be lower). Others have come to the same conclusion and conclude that taxpayer-borne risk should be priced higher than investor-borne risk. For example, Bazelon and Smetters (1999) consider that:

> In sum, there is little evidence supporting the argument that government should price risks at less than the private market. Indeed, the distorting costs of taxation and the positive long-run correlation between stocks and wages suggest that the government should possibly overprice risks relative to the private market. (p. 216)

Interestingly, and somewhat surprisingly, the strongest attack on orthodoxy on this score has come, virtually out of the blue, from Geddes and Goldman (2015), whose views have reopened the debate (Boardman and Hellowell, 2016; Moszoro, 2016). The argument of Geddes and Goldman is that the orthodox view on the lower public cost of capital fails to take account of key differences in the institutional and legal arrangements governing how private investors and taxpayers bear risks, in particular the role of limited liability and the transferability of ownership of shares. Private investors generally supply equity (residual) claims under conditions of limited liability and, in addition, the claims are normally fully transferable. By contrast, taxpayer residual claims do not include limited liability protections and are inseparable from a citizen's jurisdiction. These residual claims are inalienable and non-transferable, with taxpayers fully liable through the tax and transfer system for project losses. Both features of taxpayer residual claims – unlimited liability and non-transferability – have important implications for the cost of bearing a project's inherent risk.

   To illustrate, those authors consider an income-generating infrastructure project (e.g. a toll bridge) under both public and private financing. It generates a stream of net cash flows, which could be either positive or negative, and the residual claimants to the project's net income after covering debt service and other costs – whether taxpayers or investors – bear residual risks associated with variations in those cash flows. Private investors bear project risk through changes in the share price of their tradable residual claims. Because taxpayer residual claims cannot be traded, there is no market price for their equity exposure. Taxpayers are thus unable to capture the benefits of positive outcomes directly through increased residual claim prices, while at the same time the cost of their residual risk-bearing is unobservable.

In the event of an adverse outcome, that is, negative net cash flows, equity investors are the first to absorb losses, whether the equity investors are taxpayers or private investors. Bondholders as suppliers of debt enjoy strong contractual protections irrespective of whether a project is financed through a PPP or through more traditional financing. But, under traditional public financing, when taxpayers are residual risk bearers there is no 'cushion' provided by outside equity to absorb downside risk as under private financing. It is the absence of limited liability for taxpayers that is a key difference when comparing taxpayer risk-bearing versus risk-bearing by private investors.

Limited liability for private investors constrains the cost of capital in several ways (Geddes and Goldman, 2015, pp. 15–17). First, it caps investors' maximum exposure to losses to the amount of their investment in the enterprise, for example the project company. Second, limited liability lowers the cost of capital by allowing a diversified portfolio of investments. Under limited liability, shareholders cannot lose more than they have put in. If the securities in which investments are made are different, in the sense of being subject to different risks, the risk of loss on the portfolio as a whole must be less than the risk on any single investment. As Sir John Hicks (1983) observed, 'without limited liability this could not be done, since investment even in a second enterprise would increase the investor's risks, but with limited liability it can be' (p. 185). Where there is unlimited liability, an investor exposes his or her entire wealth even if purchasing a small stake in a large company.

In comparison, taxpayers as residual claimants of public projects do not receive limited liability protection. As a consequence, in the words of Geddes and Goldman:

> ... managers of political bodies have the unique power to impose taxes, which for these purposes can be seen as analytically analogous to the power to compel unlimited capital contributions from residual claimants. That is, where states or political subdivisions encounter fiscal difficulties, they can adjust tax rates to increase revenues to meet obligations. Furthermore, the public nature and high visibility of many large infrastructure projects make it politically difficult for officials to abandon or substantially revise projects midstream where construction costs exceed budgeted levels or where the net benefits of a project disappoint. Thus, project managers may continue to invest taxpayer funds in projects even where the predicted economic

returns do not justify such follow-on investments. If the sponsoring jurisdiction uses general revenues to subsidize the project then taxpayers are effectively contributing additional capital, and their liability via the tax system is limited only by uncertain, non-transparent political constraints. (2015, p. 17)

Further, they argue that a critical factor shaping taxpayer versus investor risk concentration is the globalization of equity, and the implications this development holds for risk spreading. The existence of a global equity market enables the risks associated with a particular firm or project to be spread rapidly to risk-bearing investors around the globe. As a result, 'private investment in a global capital market is likely to result in lower equity cost according to Arrow-Lind's risk-spreading logic' (ibid., p. 22). Such a risk-spreading option is not available to taxpayers. Non-transferability and non-tradability of taxpayers' residual claims prevents taxpayers from diversifying their public sector risk. Geddes and Goldman's conclusion is that the 'inability to use portfolio diversification – one of the most basic tools for reducing investment risk – means that the true cost of taxpayer risk bearing, and public sector borrowing, is higher than is often assumed' (ibid., p. 23).

This conclusion, however, is of little comfort to public sector procuring authorities to the extent that those supplying equity capital to the PPP are doing so under limited liability via a leveraged special purpose vehicle (SPV) project company. It highlights the importance of risk assessment for all concerned.

PPP OPTIONS

Where do PPPs go from here? Three options would seem to present themselves:

1.   abandon PPPs;
2.   take the F out of DBFOM;
3.   consider non-financial advantages of PPPs.

Abandon PPPs

This would appear to be the case in the UK where, as noted, PFI fell into disuse when it got difficult to establish that private funding provided better value than public funding. However, Charles Roxburgh, second permanent secretary to the UK Treasury, was reported as denying that the government was planning to abandon the method altogether, although the new policy enunciated does look to be a close cousin. PPPs will be used for projects where the advantage of transferring risk to the private sector outweighs the superior borrowing power of the government (The Guardian, 2018a, p. 2).

This position is broadly consistent with Officer's (2003) principle of comparative advantage in the delivery of public services, namely that the government should provide services when it is better than the market in doing so. On this basis, responsibilities would be allocated between the public sector and private sector according to which sector can add the greatest value to the community. Officer goes on to note that, on a number of scores, the government would appear to have a 'comparative disadvantage' in undertaking many business activities. Principal among these is the difficulty it has in creating incentives for managers to act in commercially oriented ways. Too often the downside risks to innovative and risk-taking activities exceed the gains, and it is easier to 'keep to the rules'. Another problem is that governments are elected with a broad mandate and this does not always translate into clear objectives. Public sector bodies are confronted with a large number of often conflicting goals, with little accountability for any of them, in an environment in which many special interest groups are clamouring for attention. Having many goals is often a recipe for achieving none of them. Frequently, especially in the past, the first stumbling block when a PPP procurement proposal is being formulated comes when the public sector entity is asked: what are the objectives of the project and what performance indicators would indicate that the aims have been achieved?

The comparative advantage rule is, in essence, the basis of the controversial value-for-money test applied under public procurement policies where private sector provision of infrastructure services under a PPP arrangement is compared against public sector provision. Many stumbling blocks are encountered and need to be overcome to be confident about the result, for example how to measure certainty equivalent, how to allow for optimism bias, and how to put a number on transferred risk. Then there is the discount rate conundrum: whether to use the actual cost of public sector financing, a rate based on social time preference, or a rate embodying a project-specific risk premium (Rebel report, 2015). While there is no simple pass or fail with this particular examination, woe betide any proposal that does not get to or fall over the line, notwithstanding all the machinations designed to do so.

To economic liberals, this presumption is the wrong way round. They would point to the Adam Smith principle that government should do only what cannot be done in the market. To do otherwise and go beyond this point, they argue, is ultimately corrosive to the market, and inhibiting to the development of free enterprise. In effect, in the words of Seldon (1990):

> the classical principle, reaffirmed by Keynes, is that government should act not where it is better than the market but only where there is no market ... Wherever, it is used, government is so disappointing or worse – inefficient, unaccountable and corrupt – that it is best not to use it at all except for functions where all its faults have to be tolerated to obtain the services required. (p. 239)

In the United States, the same principle is almost axiomatic, for PPPs must be viewed against the historical background of 'privatism' that has dominated thinking in this country since the early nineteenth century (Beauregard, 1998). Privatism is the presumption that economic activity should be left to the market; 'a belief that private institutions are intrinsically superior to public institutions for the delivery of goods and services' and 'a confidence that market efficiency is the appropriate criterion of social performance in virtually all spheres of community activity' (Barnekov et al., 1989).

Yet, in many ways, this avenue is a false trail. Who will miss out if PPPs are abandoned? If PPPs are a more efficient means of procuring and organizing infrastructure than traditional procurement then the whole community may be worse off – public assets may be less well designed, less well constructed, less well operated and less well maintained, to everyone's detriment. But not the private sector generally, for under traditional procurement methods private sector designers are likely to be used, private consulting firms may help the government to choose the best bid, private contractors will undertake the construction, private firms may be called upon to operate certain aspects, and private facilities managers are likely to be involved in the maintenance. Those who miss out are the private sector financiers, and few will shed tears for them given the financial excesses and scandals, and the absence of a moral compass, that marked the global financial crisis and the subsequent years (Lewis and Kaleem, 2019, chapter 6).

Taking Out Private Finance

One possibility is to return to full public funding of infrastructure. Having decided to finance the project itself, the government could proceed via an unbundled approach with separate contracts for design, build, operate and maintain. Construction could be commissioned by means of a fixed-price arrangement (such as design and build; engineering procurement and construction (EPC) model; or design, construct and novate) or by a managing contractor or alliance model (see Grimsey and Lewis, 2017, chapter 7 for details). Such unbundled approaches are very much of the 'this is where we came in' variety, since there are well-rehearsed arguments for and against traditional procurement. None of these arrangements can be seen as PPPs, although the alliance model can be viewed as a 'true' partnership with an 'open book' sharing of risks and rewards.

As an alternative, finance could be taken out of design, build, finance, operate, maintain (DBFOM) so that the PPP embraces design, build, operate, maintain (DBOM). Here, there is some overlap with the design and construct model except, as the name suggests, it also includes operation and maintenance activities to be undertaken once the asset has been constructed. This 'bundling' feature renders it as a type of PPP. The operation of the asset is transferred back to the client entity at the end of a specified operations and maintenance period.

The sponsoring agency manages the production of the design brief, either itself or via external consultants. Following this, the entity engages the DBOM contractor to design and construct the asset for a fixed, lump sum price, and to operate the asset and perform maintenance services for a specified period at an agreed price or on an agreed remuneration basis. The DBOM contractor does not own the asset but is contractually licensed to operate and maintain it for a specified period. The government funds the project without a capital contribution from the DBOM contractor.

The DBOM model is applicable to projects where the completed asset has some operational capacity and where the government wishes to finance the project itself, either to save time or to save cost. Nevertheless, whole-of-life efficiencies may be seen as a priority or advantage, which the DBOM provides. Benefits and disadvantages of the DBOM model are summarized in Table 4.1. Employing the DBOM model begs the question of how important the finance component is to the success of a PPP. An earlier answer by Darrin Grimsey and me (Grimsey and Lewis, 2004b) was that 'having the privately provided finance at risk acts as a catalyst to inject risk management techniques into the project in a way that is not possible under government financing' (p. 64).

While not downplaying that stance, finance is far from being the only factor at work in the PPP incentive structure (as was recognized at the time). A key feature inherent in the PPP model is the private sector management of the long-term cost and performance of major infrastructure assets. For this to happen, the private sector needs three things: control over design and construction; a payment mechanism with incentives for on-time, on-cost delivery; and financial penalties for sub-standard performance. Even in the absence of private finance, these three features remain, and with them the incentive compatibility and whole-of-life aspects of the PPP model.

Non-Financial Benefits of PPPs

Achieving value for money (VfM) has to be a prime objective for every government, whether it is itself delivering services to citizens, or undertaking the procurement and commissioning of new services on behalf of citizens. From the outset, the PPP model faced a significant challenge in that the public sector can (in most cases) borrow more cheaply from capital markets than can the private sector. In the first section of this chapter, it was argued that this position is spurious given that the PPP model internalizes risk pricing under a project finance approach whereas traditional procurement relying on government borrowing makes use of the government balance sheet and does not give a true

Table 4.1   DBOM: benefits and disadvantages

Benefits	Disadvantages
Single line of responsibility: The contractor is responsible for the design, construction, operation and maintenance of the asset, reducing the potential for disputes over design deficiencies, construction defects and delays, and operating/maintenance errors.	*Control:* The government client has less direct control over the quality and design than for a construct only or design and construct model, and has less control over the operation of the asset post-construction.
Fast track: It is possible for construction to start before the design documentation is completed.	*Client liability:* The government body may retain liability for elements of the design brief (including any preliminary design).
Administrative efficiencies: Combining the design, construction, operation and maintenance elements into one contract achieves a high level of administrative efficiencies for the client.	*Cost:* The client body may pay a premium to transfer design, construction, operation and maintenance risks to the contractor.
Limited design liability: Substantial design risk is shifted to the contractor, generally including fitness for purpose.	*Limited innovation:* The contractor has little input into the project's scope and the client's requirements, limiting opportunities for innovation.
Certainty of price: A fixed, lump sum price is payable for the design and construction of the asset, subject to limited contractually agreed adjustments. The price or remuneration basis of operation and maintenance services is fixed well before the asset is complete. This provides long-term cost certainty to the government.	*Tender period:* There is usually a longer tender period than for the construct only or design and construct models, in order to allow tenderers to assess the scope and design risks as well as the operation and maintenance risks.
Buildability: As designer and builder, the contractor has some opportunity to consider the 'buildability' of the design and create construction efficiencies.	*Cost overruns and delays:* The client body may be liable for some cost overruns and delays (as permitted under the contract).
Whole-of-life cost/quality: The contractor bears some of the whole-of-life risk and is incentivized to contemplate ongoing operating and maintenance costs in the design.	*Pool of tenderers:* The pool of potential tenderers may be reduced by combining the design, construction, operation and maintenance roles.
Operational risks: The contractor bears some or all of the operating risks (depending on the operational period and the design life of the asset).	

Source: Grimsey and Lewis (2017), p. 200.

price for the risk involved to the community (i.e. taxpayers in particular) in investing in the infrastructure project.

Nevertheless, public perceptions that the PPP model may be an expensive approach forced governments to answer the question on value by comparison with traditional procurement under the Public Sector Comparator (PSC). Notably, no other procurement model has had to pass a test of comparison with alternative models.

The VfM test against the PSC became the benchmark against which projects must pass in order to proceed as a PPP.[2] But gradually governments realized that the test is at best hypothetical and in fact most of the time unreliable. There are many reasons why this is the case and they were covered in the article 'Are Public Private Partnerships Value for Money? Evaluating Alternative Approaches and Comparing Academic and Practitioner Views' (Grimsey and Lewis, 2005b). In summary, some of the practical considerations relating to the PSC and the VfM test are:

- VfM tests are used to compare delivering an investment through a PPP with implementing it through a 'conventional' procurement approach. These analyses usually focus on the financial costs (risk-adjusted) or providing what is assumed to be an equivalent output.
- The PSC is often overly subjective and the calculation remains a hypothetical one, and the amounts are not ever put through any real market test. The PSC usually remains a statement of initial estimates, while PPP bids contain numbers to which bidders must commit contractually.
- The PSC is overly simplistic and fails to take into account the broader social ramifications that feature in a more rigorous cost–benefit analysis, for example.
- The VfM comparison is primarily a financial one between the net present values (NPVs) of the cash flows of two options. Normally, PPP guidance material also directs that the decision as to VfM should also incorporate qualitative factors. Qualitative factors by definition are not costed in the PSC as they are not accurately quantifiable.

The last two omissions are significant, because in cases where there are reasons to believe that the non-financial benefits of delivery under a PPP will be greater than under conventional procurement, standard VfM analysis is likely to underestimate the advantages of PPPs. Indeed, incentive structures built into PPP projects are specifically designed to deliver greater non-financial benefits than conventional procurements. By the term 'non-financial benefits' is meant the socio-economic benefits to service users of an infrastructure investment, including in the wider society (EPEC, 2011).

It is further argued by the European PPP Expertise Centre (EPEC) that the non-financial benefits potentially offered by PPPs are of three types:

1. Accelerated delivery (delivering services earlier).
2. Enhanced delivery (delivering services to a higher standard).
3. Wider social impacts (greater benefits to society as a whole).

These are considered in turn.

Accelerated delivery

EPEC identify two types of accelerated delivery: on-time delivery (where services start at their planned date) and earlier investment (service delivery commences earlier than would otherwise have been possible). PPPs can contribute to both.

On-time construction performance by PPPs vis-à-vis traditional procurement is largely a result of the financial incentives incorporated into the terms of PPP contracts, which apply to equity investors, lenders and contractors. Contractors are paid only when the facility is up and running, with the contracted services actually being delivered, and this feature encourages prompt delivery, if only to avoid the financial penalties for over-time delivery. Recall earlier that PPPs were described not so much as a model but as a step-by-step process guiding those using the framework to address the pertinent issues. Consequently, in practice, much of the project-specific financial and technical due diligence carried out before contract signing is focused on ensuring the best possible conditions for on-time delivery of the infrastructure. PPPs impose a contractually based structure and a set of clearly defined and agreed timescales to be met. PPP contracts can also provide clear mechanisms for dealing with variant conditions and delay events.

Having private finance available, waiting in the wings, might provide an additional source of finance that is complementary to public funds. As EPEC (2011, p. 7) says, this support could help to accelerate investment programmes. Additionally, they suggest that the long-term commitments that governments are forced to make under PPP contracts can help to focus the public sector's attention on more rational, long-term capital planning. This commitment in turn may allow the private sector to plan and deliver more coherent infrastructure programmes.

However, it seems incumbent on the VfM analysis to suggest ways in which a PPP might result in earlier availability of infrastructure investments. Certainly, at the very least, the solid record of on-time delivery of PPP projects is a pointer in that direction.

Enhanced delivery

Enhanced delivery refers to a higher level of service quality from a particular infrastructure facility, which may come about in three ways:

1. the contractual commitment to undertake maintenance should result in a better-maintained asset, enjoying a higher residual value;
2. meeting a defined service standard needs a better-designed service and delivery mechanism that limits gold-plating and responds better and faster to user needs;

3. enhanced delivery benefits derived from a clearly defined governance
    structure that enables professionals to concentrate on their core activities.

With PPPs, the fact the public sector specifies the outputs it wants, not how
to deliver the service (inputs), is aimed to facilitate innovation. PPPs that
promote innovative design generate an important economic and social value.
A well-designed hospital might help patients to get better more quickly. Given
that PPPs are long-term contracts and PPP contractors have strong incentives
to focus on the lifetime of an asset, innovation in design could lead to worthwhile returns. Furthermore, the benefits of good design in a project are not
project-specific but can be replicated in the future, including importantly in
traditional procurement.

   As an aside, this last observation should perhaps cause us to pause. Often
the comparison of PPP versus conventional procurement comes across as
some kind of tournament, fought out by proponents of PPPs and naysayers,
both defending their ground. If, however, there is a battle, it should be one to
improve procurement and thus the quality of public infrastructure. Moreover,
it is worth reiterating that since the same contractors often bid for PPP and conventionally procured projects, it is not one between public and private either,
in that there may be no skin off the noses of private sector construction firms.

   Returning to the issue of innovation, as EPEC accepts, doing something
different, or innovative, inevitably involves risk. There is a natural tendency to
avoid taking such risks unless there is a strong incentive to do otherwise. For
example, according to EPEC the public sector typically prefers to use what has
worked in the past or follow a previously selected solution as this involves less
risk. For the private partner in a PPP, including innovation in a bid could make
the difference between securing or losing a long-term contract. In this case,
there does exist an incentive to innovate. PPPs seem more likely to generate
new ways of delivering public services.[3]

   Consider again the case of hospitals. A 2010 KPMG report (in conjunction
with University College London) found that PFI hospitals have better patient
environmental ratings than conventionally procured hospitals of a comparable
age, in which facilities management services are performed either in-house or
contracted out. Also, PFI hospitals have higher cleanliness scores than non-PFI
hospitals of comparable age (KPMG, 2010).

   Benefits (financial and non-financial) also stem from better governance.
One benefit is that poorly planned projects may be sussed out and discarded
at an early juncture. A second is that the public sector is allowed to do what
it is meant to do: it focuses on outputs and policy outcomes, that is, its core
functions, and hopefully less time is spent on distracting administrative issues.
Contract management may also be enhanced, especially when the public sector
is poorly equipped to manage the integration of complex contracts. When

problems are resolved more quickly, the government is free to manage other projects, while users could expect to receive better service and attention to their concerns.

Wider social benefits
These benefits refer to positive externalities of using the PPP approach and seek to capture the benefits to persons other than the users of an asset or related service. The EPEC report found it useful to subdivide these benefits into two categories: wider public sector benefits and wider macroeconomic benefits.

Wider public sector benefits focus on the public sector and refer to the impact of a PPP beyond a specific project to the public sector in general. These comprise:

1. the benefits accruing to the public sector from a more explicit approach to cost identification and transparency;
2. the planning benefits of having long-term fixed prices and output certainty under the PPP contract; and
3. the contribution that PPPs make to improving the public sector's ability to produce projects conventionally.

There seems little doubt, at least in my mind, that the measured, deliberative, risk-based approach of PPPs has enhanced traditional procurement procedures through a demonstration effect (perhaps transitive), and narrowed the performance differences between the two approaches.

Wider macroeconomic benefits refer to the impact of an investment on the economy and environment. In particular, any innovative management practices from the private sector can be learnt and replicated in future projects, irrespective of the procurement method – which can be referred to as 'competition by comparison'. Beneficiaries are not just users of a good or asset at present, but extend to the broader public sector and economy. In this respect, PPPs have provided a fertile learning environment in which the public sector has been able to draw from best practice and apply this to more conventionally procured projects. In this case, as EPEC note, benefits come from learning by doing, applying new techniques as well as imposed systems and disciplines. These benefits are only partially captured, if at all, in the VfM evaluation process since they extend beyond the specific PPP under consideration.

In concluding this section, it is almost trite to say that the identification, quantification and valuation of non-financial benefits from PPPs is difficult to tie down and use as a counterbalance to the perceived financial disadvantages of PPPs arising from the seemingly much cheaper cost of public borrowing. Nevertheless, if there are reasons to suspect that the non-financial benefits of PPPs may exceed those of conventionally procured projects with which they are being compared, that circumstance ought not be ignored in the appraisal process.

NOTES

1. Cited in Klein (1997, p. 29).
2. For a full account see EPEC (2015).
3. In Chapter 6, the case of the Royal Adelaide Hospital in this respect is examined.

5. Why choose a PPP?

A LEADING QUESTION

In Chapter 1, attention was drawn to the criticisms of public private partner-ships (PPPs) by policymakers in the UK, especially oral evidence given by senior public officials to the House of Commons Public Accounts Committee, along with the Infrastructure and Projects Authority (IPA) (UK House of Commons Committee of Public Accounts, 2011). It was revealed that PFI fell into disuse because it became difficult to prove that private funding under the PPP gave better value than public funding. In addition, according to the chief executive of the IPA, Tony Meggs, the public sector's ability to design and construct projects on time and budget had improved. 'Therefore, the (value of) risk transfer is lower, I believe, than it was when PFIs began, because we have learned a lot along the way. Therefore, the test becomes a much higher hurdle, to prove that you are going to do much better than the public sector' (The Guardian, 2018a). As if to rub salt in the wounds, the decline in enthusiasm for PFI was such that Whitehall was unwilling to mount a defence of it.

In the light of these blows to the PPP model, and taking cognizance of the leading role that the UK market played in its development, the question that needs to be asked is: as things presently stand, what would motivate any gov-ernment to choose a PPP for public procurement?

One immediate response flows on from the comments in Chapter 1 about the likely benefits to homebuyers of the practice of 'bundling' in residential construction. There it was thought that the information asymmetries that existed between the builder and the homebuyer as to planning rules, council regulations, design concepts, engineering requirements, building techniques, materials, drainage, sewerage, finance and so on meant that an unbundled DIY approach had only limited appeal relative to a contractor organizing all of these elements and, after the necessary documentation, handing over the keys at the end.

In a broadly similar fashion, a PPP can save a government time, money and effort in the public procurement process, by consolidating many activities into one contractual arrangement. Instead of dealing with a designer/architect, arranging finance, calling for bids, selecting a contractor, overseeing construc-tion, and contracting out repairs and maintenance, a qualified contractor can be chosen to perform all or most of these functions or use their knowledge of the industry and parties involved to select a group capable of doing so (Zerunyan, 2019).

Such an arrangement draws on the comparative advantages of both partners in the PPP. The concessionaire knows who are the best architects, the most experienced contractors, the really reliable facilities managers, and so on, to draw into the team. At the same time, the public sector can focus on their core responsibilities of public safety and welfare, as well as ensuring quality delivery of public services. It is then more than likely that the public infrastructure will be suited for purpose and better maintained.

Yet, there may be many other reasons why governments might look at choosing a PPP. Here it is opportune to consider the report *PPP Motivations and Challenges for the Public Sector: Why (Not) and How* prepared by the European PPP Expertise Centre (EPEC, 2015).

MOTIVATIONS FOR PPPS

By way of preamble, the EPEC report observes that, despite the existence of a significant amount of research material on PPPs, the data are severely compromised and the quality of the information varies widely. As they say,

> Indeed there is still a lack of robust evidence from which to draw definitive conclusions, as opposed to claims, one way or the other. Many studies reflect particular interests (which may be 'for' or 'against' PPPs) and may be limited in their objectivity. Additionally, some of the research and claims made will often reflect concerns about the underlying projects and not necessarily the PPP method itself. Consequently, the report assesses the available research material to help identify the principal motivations and challenges for public authorities in implementing PPPs. (EPEC, 2015, p. 4)

By 'motivations' they mean the rationale given for the use of PPPs, while by 'challenges' the report seeks to identify potential limitations to the delivery.

In all, 15 motivations can be discerned in the report.

1. *Improve the ways in which infrastructure projects are planned, designed and constructed*

   Often PPPs are chosen for very complex projects. Significant risks are involved in the implementation of infrastructure projects, especially when there are considerable technical and engineering complications. Because of this complexity, planning, design and approval processes need to be managed carefully, taking account of all aspects of the project. PPPs can be seen as a 'process' for doing so.

2. *Provide 'insurance' against delivery and performance risks*
    Under conventional procurement methods the public sector procurer sets
    out a detailed specification of the project input (e.g. functional content
    and plan, construction design, materials to be used, civil engineering tech-
    niques to be employed) and the bearing and management of the associated
    risks. Given the right incentives, the private sector itself may be able better
    to identify and manage many of the key risks, especially of large projects.
    Any likely higher costs associated with the PPP option, relative to con-
    ventional procurement, can be viewed as a type of 'insurance premium'
    paid by the public to the private sector for the certainty of future cost and
    delivery time of the project. The question then becomes one of whether
    the cost of the PPP option is partly or fully compensated by the additional
    benefits and assurance obtained.

3. *Create incentives to engage in whole-of-life costing*
    By combining construction and long-term maintenance and management,
    a PPP embodies incentives to optimize costs over the life of the asset.
    This result is less likely in conventionally procured projects where the
    contractor is responsible for the construction of the asset but not its subse-
    quent management and maintenance. Bidders in conventionally procured
    projects may put forward technical solutions or build to a quality that may
    lower costs in the short term but lead to higher costs of maintaining or
    renewing project assets over the long term.
        By contrast, the PPP encourages the private partner to design and
    construct to achieve lower lifetime costs and to limit service interruptions
    during the operating phase of the project. A simple comparison of initial
    investment costs would not pick up these differences.

4. *Better maintained infrastructure*
    Maintenance of infrastructure is often put off or neglected during periods
    of government budget stringency. PPP contractual commitments and
    associated incentives can also be structured to ensure that there will not be
    any skimping on maintenance requirements so that the private partner will
    hand back well-maintained project assets to the procuring authority at the
    end of the contract with good (or at least better) residual value.

5. *Whole-of-life costs identified early*
    Estimated costs of the operations and maintenance phase of the PPP
    'bundle' are incorporated at the outset into the PPP bid, with the corollary
    that whole-of-life costings can be identified and evaluated before the
    public sector investment decision is made. According to EPEC, some
    thereby argue that this feature can improve decision-making by the
    public authority by ensuring that the decision whether or not to go ahead
    with a project is based on the true long-term costs of the investment.
    Conventional forms of project delivery, in which the commitment is

limited to building the asset, can ignore or downplay longer-term maintenance and operating costs. These costs may not be affordable or represent
good value. Using PPPs can be seen as a means to help overcome the
temptation for short-term thinking and ignoring problems lurking around
the corner.

6. *Better assurance of on-time, on-budget delivery*

    PPP projects generally have a better track record of on-time, on-budget
    asset delivery when compared with conventional forms of procurement.
    Moreover, depending on the specific contract, the costs of late delivery
    and being over budget are invariably 'sheeted home' (i.e. conclusively
    attributed) to the contractors. Where there is a dispute about this conse-
    quence, a cost-sharing settlement is sometimes reached.

    Included in the EPEC report is a summary of what is described as the
    'on-time, on budget' delivery of French PPPs (see Box 5.1). PPPs, of
    course, are set up with the aim of bringing about on-time and on-budget
    delivery, given that private capital is at risk with respect to the perfor-
    mance of the asset and delivery of the service in accordance with the con-
    tractually agreed time frame and performance specifications (no payment
    unless delivered satisfactorily). Further, in a PPP, the procuring authority
    has a considerable contractual commitment to the project from the start.
    This may prevent situations where conventionally procured projects
    are stopped and restarted at frequent intervals due to funding issues or
    changes in policy, resulting in higher costs and delays.[1] In fact, EPEC con-
    siders that the advantage of a PPP may be as significant as the difference
    between having a project that is delivered and having no project at all.

7. *More effective contract integration and project management*

    Project construction by means of conventional procurement likely requires
    a number of separate contracts with different contractors. This situation
    can give rise to 'interface risks' in terms of scheduling the various ele-
    ments and clarifying who is responsible for what and when to hand over
    to the next contractor. Public bodies may lack the specialist project man-
    agement skills necessary to manage these interactions, creating project
    implementation delays and cost overruns. PPPs enable contract integration
    and project management responsibilities to be transferred to the private
    partner, creating clearer and simplified lines of authority and responsibil-
    ity between the parties.

8. *Encouraging innovative designs and technologies*

    PPP contracts specify desired outputs, not inputs, a feature that allows
    greater scope for the private sector provider to decide how best to deliver
    these outputs and maximize efficiency in delivering public services.
    As a result, it is claimed that there have been changes in the design of

BOX 5.1   STUDIES OF 'ON-TIME, ON-BUDGET' DELIVERY

With the endorsement of MAPPP (Mission d'appui aux partenariats public-privé), the central government PPP unit in France, a study was carried out in 2011 on a sample of 34 PPP projects in France that had reached financial close since 2004. The findings were as follows:

- On time – not taking into account changes requested by the procuring authority, 79 per cent of PPP projects were delivered within the contractually agreed timetable. Conditional payments to the private partner were seen as a strong driver in achieving this. The main reasons for delays were changes required by the procuring authority, changes in legislation and delays in obtaining permits.
- On budget – 47 per cent of the projects that were tendered as PPPs had cost overruns. In most of the cases the main reason for cost overruns was linked to variations required by the procuring authority (55 per cent of the cases). However, most of the additional costs (80 per cent) were limited to 3 per cent of the initial budget, and only 7 per cent overran the budget by 10 per cent or more.

Source: EPEC (2015), based on *Etude sur la performance des contrats de partenariat* – PWC France (2011).

buildings or the use of new technologies, producing long-term operational efficiencies. Since some PPP contractors straddle a number of markets, PPPs have been effective in attracting into the market a wider range of skills, technologies and approaches from the global private sector.

9. *Better asset maintenance over time*

    Putting off maintenance can erode the quality of the infrastructure and the services it provides to the community. Where maintenance and life-cycle investment is part of the 'bundle', PPPs provide a degree of certainty and discipline that adequate and timely maintenance will be carried out. This is because the private partner is contractually obliged to do so and the procuring authority is contractually obliged to pay for it.

10. *Consistency of service delivery*

    Policymakers and procuring authorities cite the benefits that flow from PPP payment mechanisms. In particular, the requirement in a PPP for performance-based measurement of service operations can mitigate against any decline in quality and assist in ensuring consistency in the level and quality of services being delivered over the long term.

11. *Payments for infrastructure services spread over time*

Payments under a PPP are analogous to a rental agreement and charges for the use of a car, rather than buying the car outright at the beginning. In much the same way, PPP projects can spread the cost of paying for infrastructure over the lifetime of the asset. By bringing forward and spreading payment over time, PPPs allow projects to take place that might not otherwise be possible to undertake due to budget constraints. Proponents argue that in this way a PPP can allow the benefits of a project to be delivered sooner, even if they still eventually have to be paid for over the longer term. Thus, like rentals, PPPs can enable projects to be brought forward. At the same time, payments for services are aligned with benefits received.

12. *Certainty of costs*

With a PPP contract in place, the procuring agency will be able to rely on a high degree of certainty as to the cost it will incur over the life of the project. This is because the costs of construction, operation and maintenance are largely determined and contracted for up front. Further, any increases in capital, operating or maintenance costs for the agreed service provision will, in most circumstances, fall on the private partner. A PPP can consequently provide a higher level of certainty on the long-term costs and budget impact of projects than other forms of public procurement.

13. *Involvement of lenders and others can bring in extra 'eyes'*

PPPs are able to expose projects to broad upfront scrutiny by lenders, equity investors and subcontractors, limiting the risk of the procuring authority entering into contracts for unjustified or poorly structured or monitored projects. Since their capital will be exposed to the performance risk of the project, financiers can be expected to carry out a significant amount of due diligence on the project, especially if they are required to bear demand risk, and they will want to be assured that users are prepared to pay for the service. This assessment is usually carried out by lenders with the support of independent expert advisers (e.g. technical, legal, financial, insurance). Yet, it must be said, forecasting demand is not easy, and there are many 'slips between the cup and the lip' as the old adage warns.

14. *Private finance as a driver for project performance*

It is also argued that because private capital only receives a return on the condition that the project performs in line with the contractually agreed performance standards, a strong incentive is created to ensure the performance of the project is on time and on budget. Consequently, the interests of private capital are aligned with those of the public sector to ensure sound performance. As EPEC argues, private investors and lenders are not forgiving towards contractors or operators who deliver late, overrun on costs or deliver poor operational performance if this threatens project revenues due to deductions in availability payments or low usage. Such incentives and the alignment of interests depend on the terms of the PPP agreement, establishing that finance is genuinely subject to performance risk and that the agreement is properly enforced.

15. *Who bears the burden of debt?*

All PPP projects have to be paid for at some point. Two sources of cash ultimately bear the cost of funding projects: taxpayers (whose taxes enable governments, for example, to make availability payments on their behalf) or users (who may, for example, pay a toll to use a highway). Financing, on the other hand, is money that must be paid back (e.g. loans or equity from the public or private sector). Finance is used to bridge the gap between project inception, when funding may not be sufficient, and later when resources are eventually available to pay for the project. In this respect, borrowing – that is, financing – shifts the repayment from the present generation of users or taxpayers to later generations (Buchanan, 1958, 1992). This is irrespective of the method of procurement.

User-pay PPPs (concessions) link the provision of the benefit of the investment directly to those who receive and pay for the benefit. In the case of toll roads, user-pay PPPs might be seen as a fairer way to allocate the burden of funding and of distributing the benefits of infrastructure among existing citizens, although interpersonal and intergenerational issues remain. For example, all of society, not just current users, benefit from infrastructure, while future generations benefit from assets funded by today's users.

CHALLENGES FOR PPPS

Having reviewed the motivations for choosing PPPs most frequently advanced by public sector stakeholders, the EPEC report then goes on to consider the commonly observed challenges when implementing a PPP agenda.

1. *Institutional requirements are considerable*

A common complaint about PPPs is that they are more complex and time-consuming to procure and manage than conventional forms of procurement. The report goes on to add that, in some cases, this criticism can be misplaced once it is recognized that the existing conventional approaches themselves may be in need of improvement. However, in other cases, the complaints about PPPs may reflect genuine constraints in the policy, legal and institutional framework.

Two things stand out. First, since PPPs require a commitment over 20–30 years, say, a PPP programme will not be viable without a strong and stable political environment. Otherwise, if everything is to change with the next political cycle, private sector partners cannot be expected to spend significant time and money preparing, investing in and implementing projects.

Second, because PPPs are based on the foundation of a legal commitment, they require a supportive and effective legal framework, due to the public procurement processes involved and the heavy dependence of them on the use of contracts among the various parties.

2. *PPPs are often linked to the privatization or outsourcing of public services*

Equating them is a common error. As noted in Chapter 2, the extensive involvement of the private sector in PPPs is not the same as privatization, as the procured infrastructure is not turned over to private ownership permanently. Nor is a PPP the same as outsourcing, due to the length of the contract and the degree of commitment. Operationally speaking, two things make a PPP different from privatization: regulation of the PPP is through the contract, not the market; and the lack of government disengagement. Nevertheless, when the operation and maintenance of the facility is turned over to the private entity for 20–30 years, say, many would see this transfer as akin to privatization. Formally it isn't, but it might be regarded as a close relation.

3. *Is it acceptable to have the private sector providing public services?*

Although not really engaged in privatization either overtly or by stealth, PPPs do not receive a good press. In part, this is because the public does not understand how PPPs work, and often nor do journalists. For others, there is debate about the protection of the rights of public sector workers. If so, that can apply in the case of privatization or outsourcing, which can displace the jobs of government workers. However, by and large, only private sector firms and workers are employed in the detailed design and construction of infrastructure, whether by traditional procurement or by PPPs.

A related issue raised by EPEC is the acceptability of the private sector generating profits from the provision of public services. For some, all profits are unacceptable. Hollywood star Russell Brand, interviewed by Jeremy Paxman on the BBC on 25 October 2013 stated: 'I think the very concept of profit should be hugely reduced. David Cameron [UK Prime Minister at the time] said profit isn't a dirty word, I say profit is a filthy word.'[2]

EPEC observes that not all PPPs are successful and may have been deployed poorly. This can lead to the 'sound of failure' being louder than the 'sound of success', which can in turn lead to opposition to the use of PPPs. Profit-generating PPPs are damned if they do, and damned if they don't. Even in mature PPP markets, a shared understanding and acceptance of PPPs may be lacking.

In South Australia, my home state, the most expensive public hospital in the world was built under a PPP contract. Yet, many do not know that it is a PPP, thinking it is just another government project. I discuss this case further in Chapter 6.

4. *What services to include in the bundle?*

Another question, not directly discussed by EPEC, is what services to incorporate into the bundle. The veritable 'alphabet soup' of PPP acronyms indicates that there is a wide choice, for example BLT (build, lease, transfer), BLTM (build, lease, transfer, maintain), BTO (build, transfer, operate), BOOR (build, own, operate, remove), BOOT (build, own, operate, transfer), LROT (lease, renovate, operate, transfer), DBFO (design, build, finance, operate), DCMF (design, construct, manage, finance), DBOM (design, build, operate, maintain) and DBFOM (design, build, finance, operate, maintain). Whether or not to include private finance (i.e. the choice between the last two) has already been discussed in the preceding chapter, along with my disagreement with those who focus on the raw numbers, and the apparently much lower cost of government borrowings, and not their economic meaning and implications. Governments can of course access cheaper finance than the private sector, but will bear more risk in the process, which to an economist cannot be ignored.

Another issue is the inclusion of maintenance. The significance of whole-of-life costing does depend considerably on the type of project. On the basis of the example of an 'exemplar' hospital offering full acute services, Wright et al. (2019) conclude:

> The capital cost is small relative to the total life-cycle costs, and so are the costs to run the building services (hard and soft FM). The only thing that really matters is the costs of providing the clinical services – this is mostly labour … [A]ssuming that the design and the construction of the hospital are appropriate, the costs incurred in developing the facility are then relatively immaterial. Equally, the maintenance costs of the hospital are not large – in present value terms, they are a little less than the capital costs. But the medical costs are ten times the size of either; this is what the economics of a service-intensive activity look like. An asset like a road would have a very different life-cycle pattern: dominated even in NPV terms by the construction cost. (p. 142)

5. *Public sector capacity to deliver projects*

Obviously, as was noted above (#1), it is important to have the right institutional framework (policy, legal) in place to support PPPs. In addition, a major source of constraint can be weaknesses in the capacity and processes to deliver PPPs within these frameworks. Preparation, procurement and management of PPP contracts can be a complex and resource-intensive undertaking for a procuring authority. A range of different skills are also needed throughout the project cycle. A lack of capacity can affect PPPs at all stages of the project cycle, from initial analysis through to long-term management of the contract.

6. *Perhaps the problem lies with PPPs*

There is no doubt that PPPs are complex, and they may be considered too complex for the public sector to deliver. However, the issue may not necessarily be one of greater complexity, but of different complexities. While PPPs may involve complexities of preparing, financing, procuring and managing performance-based contracts, they also hand over to the private sector complexities such as design, construction and maintenance of infrastructure, which the private sector may be better suited to manage. Matters can be further compounded by resistance or inertia within the public sector to new and unfamiliar processes and approaches (such as developing contracts on an output rather than input basis). There is also often political pressure to get projects underway more quickly than is feasible, without recognizing the time and skills required adequately to prepare and procure them as PPPs.

7. *Managing the PPP process*

Even if the legal framework is adequate and there is potential access to the necessary skills within government, another constraint can be a lack of clearly defined powers and processes in the public sector for the effective management of the various phases of PPP project development. Recognizing that PPP procurement is essentially a project management undertaking, a number of countries have developed public sector project management approaches and processes. Importantly, these begin with a focus on the specialized project delivery team and how it is organized to ensure clarity with respect to roles, responsibilities, powers and accountabilities.

8. *Are PPPs too onerous?*

Putting in place special additional processes for PPPs may be viewed as erecting barriers to their use and creating disincentives to putting forward proposals for PPPs. If, as compared to conventional procurement, PPPs are such a problem, why bother? Answering this question is another of the 'this is where I came in' variety. Yet, it does raise questions as to whether alternative forms of project delivery are subject to the same level of scrutiny in assessing, preparing and procuring projects, and if not, why not.

Are PPPs merely a focused technical addition to procurement options? Does this broadening of the arsenal introduce features that cannot be obtained otherwise? Treating PPP procurement as one of a number of procurement options may also help to ensure that the PPP process is not more or less onerous than other public investment processes. It may also encourage good project delivery approaches which are then applied equally to all projects.

9. *Are the cards stacked against PPPs?*
   EPEC follow up the last observation above by questioning the disparity of treatment of PPPs versus conventional procurement. In order to justify the choice of the PPP option, procuring authorities are usually required to estimate the benefits of the PPP option relative to conventional procurement approaches at an early stage in a project's preparation. For example, PPP policy in Australia requires a Public Sector Comparator (PSC) to be developed for all PPPs as a way of testing whether the PPP gives better value for money (VfM) than traditional procurement methods.

   However, in many cases, the choice of a conventional approach does not have to be justified in comparison to a PPP approach. Thus, the PPP route may involve an additional process not required for other approaches. Furthermore, the analysis usually depends on making assumptions about the future, such as expected future costs and benefits. By their nature these assumptions are open to challenge. In addition, not only are reliable data limited, but the methods of analysing this information, such as discounting and probability analysis, can be complex and open to debate, especially with respect to transferred risk calculations. PricewaterhouseCoopers (PWC), in its 2017 report *Reimagining Public Private Partnerships*, notes that the PSC as a pass/fail test was abandoned by the Victorian, New South Wales and Australian Capital Territory governments, and other states in Australia are following their lead (PWC, 2017).

10. *Determining an appropriate allocation of risks*
    Shifting risks to the private sector is an attraction of PPPs. Yet, for risks that are better managed by the public partner, this effort leads to less interest from the private sector in the PPP project or may even make the project 'un-bankable' for financiers. If such risks are borne by the private party, this may lead to higher costs than necessary to manage such risks, or even to failure of the PPP. Similarly, allocating risks to the public sector that are better managed by the private sector may not maximize the potential VfM.

    Two examples stand out from those identified by EPEC. First, projects involving major tunnelling and significant geological/archaeological uncertainties are especially hazardous and will not normally be suitable for PPPs unless adequate risk-sharing arrangements are adopted, such as 'cost-plus' alliance constructs. Second, transferring demand risk to the private sector has to be carefully evaluated, as (1) demand will depend on a wide range of economic factors, (2) infrastructure pricing is very much set by public policy (i.e. outside of the private partner's control) and

(3) time and time again, private contractors overestimate latent demand and underestimate the impact of tolls in reducing customer demand. The performance of PPPs based on demand (e.g. toll road concessions) has proven to be mixed around the world.

11. *Inflexibility*

PPPs are frequently criticized for their inflexibility, inability to accommodate change, and for locking procurers into services which are difficult and costly to change. To the extent that these matters should have been identified at the outset, this outcome suggests poorly prepared PPP contracts, poor management of the contract, technological developments, major changes in requirements or policy or, more fundamentally, the inappropriate use of the proposed form of PPP in relation to the nature of the services. PPPs are usually best used where the long-term service requirements are predictable and stable and limited technological changes are expected. Ultimately, there has to be a trade-off between flexibility and whole-of-life costing. Complex flexibility provisions erode the advantages of upfront whole-of-life costing.

12. *The 'Goldilocks' problem*

The size of the project can be a challenge for PPPs. PPP projects usually need to be of a certain minimum size to justify the extensive (often fixed) transaction costs that are involved during the procurement phase (e.g. bid preparation, negotiations, advisers' costs) and attract the interest of bidders and associated financing. By contrast, projects that are large can also face constraints in the financing and contracting pool available. Very large projects may present additional challenges if a contractor subsequently fails and needs to be replaced. Suggestions that small projects can be combined to make a large one, or that large projects can be arbitrarily split up to better suit the needs of the PPP, are unrealistic. The reality is that infrastructure projects themselves are highly idiosyncratic, and PPPs have to adjust to that fact, not the other way round. No project size is 'just right'.

13. *The cost of finance again*

The EPEC report draws attention to an issue that was raised earlier in this volume, namely that the cost of private finance in a PPP is typically higher than that at which the public sector can borrow and that this would appear to undermine the rationale for using a PPP. EPEC's response is that the financing cost differential mainly reflects the fact that the private partner is assuming certain risks in a PPP that would otherwise be left with the procuring authority. That is, the private party is taking on the costs of managing such risks which would otherwise be a cost that the public sector, and ultimately the taxpayer, would have to bear.

CONCLUDING COMMENTS

This chapter has been considering the question of why, given the trenchant criticisms made of PPPs as outlined in Chapter 1, a procuring public agency would put these issues aside and choose to use a PPP for the provision of public services. The initial answer offered continued the earlier analysis of bundling – the defining characteristic of a PPP. There must presumably be cost savings and economies in scale and scope in dealing with one, all embracing, contract rather than many different contracts when engaging the separate service providers.

Attention then shifted to the EPEC report on the topic, which reviewed a wide range of motivations, drawing on the reasons most frequently put forward by public authorities and stakeholders in implementing PPPs. Altogether, based on that analysis, 15 factors motivating the choice of PPPs could be discerned, ranging in no particular order from managing the planning and approval processes, to the complexity of construction and operation, achieving whole-of-life costing incentives, obtaining 'insurance' against delivery delays and over-budget cost performance, offering incentives to innovate, preventing funding shortages, better maintenance of facilities, better contract integration, enabling costs of paying for infrastructure services to be spread over time in line with benefits, long-term certainty of costs, identifying costs earlier, contractors being paid only when infrastructure assets are delivered and operating to an agreed standard, creating 'contestability' in public infrastructure provision, and drawing in extra 'eyes' to assess project worthiness and clarifying who ultimately benefits from and pays for the infrastructure.

Then, the challenges faced in implementing and delivering a PPP agenda were considered. Again, a large number emerged, in all 13 being canvassed. Many of the factors identified arose because, as was mentioned earlier, PPPs should not be seen as a model that can be unloaded and put straight to work, but as a process to guide public procurers and decision-makers through step-by-step procedures that will hopefully bring about better risk allocation, better value, better whole-of-life costing and better certainty of outcomes.

Nowhere are the challenges for PPPs, indeed for all procurement models, greater than in the case of megaprojects, and the issues involved are taken up in the next chapter.

NOTES

1. Witness, for example, the long delays in conventionally procured Greek motorways, discussed in Chapter 1.
2. Recalled in *The Australian*, 4 March 2019. The report also recorded that Russell Brand was worth an estimated $15 million.

6.   PPPs and megaprojects

INTRODUCTION

This chapter examines megaprojects and, in particular, the decision-making problems that beset them. It is informed by three sources. First, there is the pathbreaking research by Bent Flyvbjerg and his co-authors, most notably as reported in Flyvbjerg et al. (2002 and 2003). Their worldwide studies documented the significant gap between estimated and actual costs in large projects, and put the term 'megaproject' at the forefront of infrastructure analysis. Second, the next influence is my book on Ponzi schemes (Lewis, 2015). Researching it brought to my attention the field of behavioural economics and the insights it offered into the all-too-common flaws in decision-making. Third, later work on behavioural economics suggested other problems and biases in decision-making, for example 'motivated reasoning' (Epley and Gilovich, 2016).

What the chapter seeks to do is to review and integrate this material and, building on Grimsey and Lewis (2017), craft a narrative on the issues involved in megaprojects, before focusing specifically upon PPP megaprojects.

MEGAPROJECTS AND THEIR CHARACTERISTICS

What exactly is a megaproject? Flyvbjerg (2014) defines them as 'large-scale, complex investments that typically cost a billion dollars and up' (p. 1). Frick (2008), drawing on Altshuler and Luberoff (2003), considers that 'megaprojects typically cost at least $250 million to $1 billion' (p. 240). However, $1 billion appears to be the norm (Little, 2011), these of course being US dollars.

According to the European Cooperation in Science and Technology, as cited in Wikipedia (2019), megaprojects are characterized both by extreme complexity (both in technical and human terms) and by a long record of poor delivery'(p. 11). Time delays and cost overruns seem to be commonplace. Inaccurate forecasts of the demand for the infrastructure services, resulting in severe revenue shortfalls on infrastructure investments, have led to descriptions such as 'appraisal optimism' and 'optimism bias' that are now embedded into procurement manuals and training courses.

Table 6.1   *Differences between actual and estimated costs in large*
                  public works transport projects

Project type	Original database 1927–98		Enlarged database[1] 1927–2009	
	Number of projects	Average cost escalation (%)*	Number of projects	Average cost escalation (%)*
Rail	58	44.7 (38.4)	195	34.1 (43.5)
Fixed-link[2]	33	33.8 (62.4)	743	32.8 (58.2)[3]
Road	167	20.4 (29.9)	537	19.8 (31.4)
All projects	258	27.6 (38.7)	806	24.5 (n/a)

Notes:
* Figures in brackets are the standard deviation of the cost inaccuracies.
[1] Includes original database.
[2] Fixed-link projects consist of tunnels and bridges.
[3] Data combine 38 bridges, average cost escalation 30.3% (60.6); and 36 tunnels, average cost escalation 35.5% (56.3).
Sources: Based on data in Flyvbjerg et al. (2002) and Cantarelli et al. (2012).

In 2002, the Danish study by Flyvbjerg et al. examined 258 large transport infrastructure projects covering 20 countries, the overwhelming majority of which were developed using conventional approaches to public procurement.[1] Costs were found to be underestimated in 90 per cent of the cases. For rail projects actual costs are on average 45 per cent higher than estimated, for tunnels and bridges actual costs are on average 34 per cent higher, while for road projects actual costs averaged 20 per cent higher than estimated. The authors also find no evidence that this position has changed over the past 70 years. Table 6.1, on the left-hand side, summarizes the overall results from their study.

Usefully, the original database, covering the years 1927 to 1998, was later extended, as reported by Cantarelli et al. (2012), and the results from the larger database of 806 projects are summarized on the right-hand side of Table 6.1. Note that the original database of 258 transport projects is encompassed within the enlarged database, which now runs from 1927 to 2009 and covers 17 identified countries and 'several unspecified countries' (ibid., p. 7). For this extended analysis, fixed links are broken down into tunnels and bridges, but the main change is the considerably lower average cost overrun for rail projects, while the average cost overrun for road projects is little changed. In view of the larger sample examined, it would seem that cost overruns in transport infrastructure projects are a 'global phenomenon' (ibid., p. 2), although the authors accept that 'the current sample of 806 projects is probably not representative of the population of transport infrastructure projects' (ibid., p. 8), having what they believe to be a conservative bias.

'THE IRON LAW'

Grimsey and Lewis (2017) noted that, in a follow-up analysis, Flyvbjerg (2014) summarized the current evidence with respect to megaprojects, as set out below. The features that he emphasized are typically 'overlooked or glossed over when ... [t]he megaproject format is chosen for the delivery of large scale ventures' (p. 3).

1. *Risk.* Due to long planning horizons and complex interfaces, megaprojects are inherently risky (Flyvbjerg, 2006).
2. *Leadership.* Projects are often led by planners and managers without deep project experience who keep changing throughout the long project cycles that apply to megaprojects, leaving leadership weak.
3. *Decision-making.* Decision-making, planning and management are invariably processes involving a large number of stakeholders, public and private, frequently with conflicting interests (Aaltonen and Kujala, 2010).
4. *Idiosyncracity.* Technology and designs are usually non-standard, leading to what is termed 'uniqueness bias' among planners and managers, who tend to see their projects as distinctive, mitigating against learning from other projects.
5. *Political prestige.* Overcommitment of political prestige to a project concept at an early stage results in 'lock-in' or 'capture', blunting analysis of alternatives and leading to escalated commitment in later stages. 'Fail fast' does not apply; 'fail slow' does (Cantarelli et al., 2010).
6. *Rent-seeking.* Because of the vast sums of money involved, agency problems and rent-seeking behaviour are common, as is optimism bias (Flyvbjerg, 2009).
7. *Contract variations.* The project scope will often change significantly over time, leading to overreaching and overambitious design and scope variations.
8. *Uncertainty.* Delivery is a high-risk, stochastic activity, with overexposure to 'disaster scenarios' with massive consequences (Taleb, 2010). Managers tend to ignore the possible uncertain outcomes, treating projects as if they exist largely in a deterministic world of cause, effect and control.[2]
9. *No buffer.* Statistical evidence shows that unplanned events and complexities are often unaccounted for, leaving budgets and time profiles exposed.
10. *Information failures.* Misinformation about costs, schedules, benefits and risks is the norm throughout project development and decision-making, with the result being cost overruns, delays and benefit shortfalls that undermine project viability during project implementation and operations.

In terms of the last point, that is, the extent of cost overruns, time delays and benefit shortfalls, Flyvbjerg (2014) observes that in fact nine out of ten megaprojects experience cost overruns. Moreover, cost overrun is a problem in private as well as public sector projects, and matters do not seem to be improving, as overruns have stayed large and constant for the 70-year period of the original database, and remain in the enlarged dataset (Table 6.1 above). Geography also does not seem to matter, and all countries and continents for which data are available suffer from overruns. Similarly, benefit shortfalls of up to 50 per cent are also common, and above 50 per cent is not unusual, again with no signs of improvements over time and geography (Flyvbjerg et al., 2002). For example,

> ... for rail projects an average cost overrun of 44.7 per cent combines with an average demand shortfall of 51.4 per cent, and for roads, an average cost overrun of 20.4 per cent combines with a 50:50 risk that demand is also wrong by more than 20 per cent. With errors and biases of such magnitude in the forecasts that form the basis for business cases, cost–benefit analyses, and social and environmental impact assessments, such analyses will also, with a high degree of certainty, be strongly misleading. (Flyvbjerg, 2014, p. 5)

If success in megaproject planning and management is identified as projects being delivered on budget, on time and with expected benefits, then the evidence assembled by Flyvbjerg and his co-researchers indicates that approximately one out of ten megaprojects is on budget, one out of ten is on schedule, and one out of ten is on benefits, and therefore approximately one in a thousand projects is a success, defined as on target for all three. Even if the numbers are wrong by a factor of two – so that two, instead of one, out of ten projects are on target for cost, schedule and benefits respectively – the success rate would still be dismal, now eight in a thousand. This serves to illustrate what Flyvbjerg goes on to call the 'iron law of megaprojects': over budget, over time, over and over again (ibid., p. 5). On these figures, it would appear that success is the rarity, and failure is the norm.

Although much evidence has been drawn from transport megaprojects, the 'iron law' would also appear to apply to other megaprojects, as illustrated by Flyvbjerg et al. (2003) with respect to the Suez Canal, Sydney Opera House and Concorde, and I would add also from the Mott MacDonald (2002) study commissioned by the UK Treasury examining the outcomes of 50 large UK engineering projects over the previous 20 years (see Grimsey and Lewis, 2004b). A relatively recent example comes from another infrastructure sector. At the end of 2016, according to the World Nuclear Industry Status Report, an independent annual assessment, there were 54 nuclear reactors under construction in 13 nations, and 33 are badly delayed, most particularly those employing the European Pressurized Reactor (EPR) and the Westinghouse AP1000 technologies. Unexpected problems, missteps and supply chain issues have afflicted these nuclear projects which employed the new technologies, and which contracted out work to global engineering firms (Smith and Narioka, 2016; The Economist, 2017).

OVERCOMING THE PLANNING FALLACY

Appraisal optimism has long been recognized as being the greatest danger in transport investment analysis (Mackie and Preston, 1998). They contend that it happens because the information contained in the appraisal tends to be generated or commissioned by scheme promoters who have obvious incentives to bias the results – knowingly or unconsciously – in one or more ways that inflate benefits or understate costs, factors expanded on by Flyvbjerg and his co-authors below. Such behaviour is seen by Mackie and Preston to be a particularly acute problem if the scheme is in the public domain rather than in the private sector, since the normal commercial checks and balances on excessive optimism do not apply.

However, in situations where planners and politicians endeavour to make forecasts accurate they are confronted by what Kahneman and Tversky (1979) called the 'planning fallacy'. This term is used to describe plans and forecasts that are unrealistically close to best-case scenarios and could be improved by consulting the statistics of similar cases (Kahneman, 2011, p. 250). Kahneman goes on to note that examples of the planning fallacy abound in the experiences of individuals, governments and businesses, and gives a number of illustrations.

One such illustration is based on the analysis of Flyvbjerg et al. (2005) of rail projects undertaken worldwide between 1969 and 1998. In more than 90 per cent of the cases the number of passengers projected to use the system was overestimated. Even though these passenger shortfalls were widely publicized, the evidence indicates that forecasts did not improve over those 30 years. On average, planners overestimated how many people would use the new rail projects by a whopping 100 per cent. In addition, the average cost overrun was 45 per cent. As more evidence accumulated, the experts did not become more reliant upon it.

A second, dare one say more homely, example comes from house renovations. In 2002, a survey of American homeowners who had remodelled their kitchens found that, on average, they had expected the job to cost $18 658. In fact, they ended up paying an average price of $38 769 (Survey of American Homeowners, 2002).

Unwarranted optimism on the part of planners and decision-makers seems a likely cause in both cases. Yet, it may not be the only factor. Errors in the initial budgeting and costings are not always innocent. Building contractors and kitchen renovators operating on fixed-price contracts candidly admit to researchers (though not to their customers) that they routinely make most of their profit on variations to the original plan. In these cases, the failures of forecasting reflect the inability of clients to imagine how much their ambitions for the project, driven by contractors' inducements, will escalate over time, rather than instead making a realistic plan and sticking to it.

Furthermore, authors of unrealistic plans are often driven by the desire to get the schemes approved, whether by their bosses or by the procurer, comforted by the knowledge that projects are rarely abandoned unfinished merely because of overruns in cost or completion times. Then there is the sunk-cost fallacy (Arkes and Blumer, 1985), and the unwillingness to abandon ventures in which so much intellectual or emotional energy has been invested. As Kahneman says, in such cases the greatest responsibility for avoiding the planning fallacy lies with the decision-makers who endorse the plan. Not recognizing the need for an independent outside view is a planning fallacy.

The proposed solution for the planning fallacy has now acquired a technical name, 'reference class forecasting', a method originally developed to compensate for the type of cognitive bias in human forecasting that Daniel Kahneman found in his Nobel Prize-winning work on bias in economic forecasting (Kahneman and Tversky, 1979; Kahneman, 1994). Reference class forecasting has found a strong advocate in Flyvbjerg (2006) as well as in Kahneman (2011).

Using distributional information from other ventures similar to that being forecasted is called taking an 'outside view', as a cure to the planning fallacy. Such an outside view is implemented by using a sufficiently large database, which provides information on both plans and outcomes for hundreds of projects all over the world, and can be used to provide statistical information about the likely overruns of cost and time, and about the likely underperformance of projects of different types. Note that the outside view does not try to forecast the specific events that will affect the particular project, but instead places the project in a statistical distribution of outcomes from a group of reference projects.

In broad terms, reference class forecasting requires the following three steps be taken for the individual project in hand:

1. Identify an appropriate reference class (kitchen renovations, hospitals, large railway projects and so on).
2. Obtain the statistics of the reference class (in terms of cost per mile of railway, cost per bed of hospitals, or of the percentage by which expenditures exceeded budget). Use the statistics to generate a baseline prediction.
3. Compare the specific project with the reference class distribution, in order to establish the most likely outcome for the specific project.

Unfortunately, searching out and gathering information about related cases does not seem to be part of the planner's normal toolkit, which is why Grimsey and Lewis (2009) suggested instead the value of examining benchmark projects. Further, the comparative advantage of the outside view is most pronounced for non-routine projects, that is, projects that planners and decision-makers in a certain locale have never attempted before. It is in the evaluation of such new ventures that the biases towards optimism and inaccuracy are likely to be the greatest. However, it seems possible that the outside view, being based on prior precedent, may fail to predict extreme outcomes, that is, those that lie outside all historical patterns. But for most projects, the outside view seems likely to produce more accurate results (Flyvbjerg, 2008).

BEHAVIOURAL ECONOMICS INSIGHTS

Nevertheless, matters do not always proceed in this calculated way. In the standard rational model of economics, people take risks because the odds are favourable: they accept some probability of a costly failure because the probability of success is sufficient. Instead, because the tendency towards optimism seems almost unavoidable, Kahneman advanced an alternative theory of decision-making in which optimistic bias is a significant source of risk-taking (Lovallo and Kahneman, 2003). Behavioural economics recognizes that there are systematic biases that arise when people form beliefs and make decisions (Barberis and Thaler, 2003; Thaler, 2016):

- *Overconfidence.* People are overconfident in their judgements. This appears in two guises. The confidence intervals people assign to their estimates of project and investment returns are far too narrow. People are also poorly calibrated when estimating probabilities: events they think are certain to occur actually occur only around 80 per cent of the time, and events they deem 'impossible' occur approximately 20 per cent of the time. In appropriate doses, confidence itself can be a valuable attribute: hope and confidence are generally preferable to anguish and uncertainty. Also, confidence in one's ability and chances of success is a powerful motivator to undertake long-term projects and persevere with them, and helps to convince others to come along. Yet, excessive overconfidence is quite dangerous, as the beliefs which underpin it can be resistant to many forms of evidence, leading to wishful thinking and reality denial.
- *Optimism.* Most people display unrealistically rosy views of their abilities and prospects (Weinstein, 1980). Typically, over 90 per cent of those surveyed think they are above average in their ability to get along with people and to pick winners. They also display a systematic planning fallacy, pre-

dicting that tasks (such as writing a book) will be completed much sooner than they actually are (Buehler et al., 1994).

- *Belief perseverance.* Once people have formed an opinion and made a decision, they cling to it too tightly and for too long (Lord et al., 1979). At least two factors appear to be at work. One is that people are reluctant to search for evidence that contradicts their beliefs. The other is that, even if they find such evidence, they treat it with excessive scepticism.

In this context, psychologists have recognized the existence of 'confirmation bias', a type of selective thinking whereby individuals (or groups) tend to take note of, and search out, information that confirms their beliefs and to ignore, not look for and undervalue the relevance of that which contradicts their beliefs (Gilovich, 1991; Mascarenhas, 2009; Zweig, 2009). Because of these psychological pitfalls, it is easy for investors (and advisers) to rationalize and focus attention on data that support the hypothesis or proposal rather than to seek out, and assess with an open mind, evidence that might disprove it. Warning signals are ignored and critical faculties are suspended.

In addition, biased information processing can readily permeate a social setting, such as a board meeting or a government development policy committee meeting. Specifically, a 'groupthink' mentality can develop where no one wants to be the one to challenge the supposed all-knowing, convincing chairman or leader behind the idea, and puncture the basis of the project operation. Janis (1980) coined the term 'groupthink' to refer to a process in which individually intelligent people, when in a certain group context, convince each other of the rightness of what turns out to be a foolish course of action. This result is attributed by Stephen Greenspan (2009, p. 56) to two shared illusions: an illusion of invulnerability (how could such a smart collection of people fail to make the correct decision?); and an illusion of unanimity (there is usually never any critical questioning of the group's decision or any willingness to open up the discussions to consider possible alternatives).

Reinforcing such attitudes, where members of the planning group share a bond due to their affinity to the project, the existence of the affinity grouping makes it awkward for other members to raise the hard questions that should be asked before a decision is taken. In a precursor to his work on cognitive dissonance (Festinger, 1957), Festinger, in 1950, examined group dynamics and what he called 'pressures to uniformity' (Festinger, 1950). When differences of opinion arise within a group, a discernible tension develops that group members seek to resolve. That tension, he maintained, is diminished only when agreement is achieved, typically by the majority pressuring the minority to go along with them.

Bénabou and Tirole (2016) refer to a 'psychological multiplier' and the possibility of multiple social cognitions. That is, groups or organizations can operate either in a realistic model where everyone faces the facts as they are, or in a delusional mode in which everyone engages in denial of bad news, which in turn makes things worse for everyone else. Bénabou (2013) argues that such 'groupthink' is more likely, first, when co-dependency among group members is high, that is, they share a largely common fate, with few exit options from the collateral damage inflicted by others' mistakes; and second, when the adverse state of the world is relatively rare, but when it occurs is really bad – a so-called 'black swan' event.

By these means, when forecasting the outcomes of risky projects, there are mental traps into which people can fall, and decision-makers too readily can become victim to the planning fallacy. Under its sway, they make decisions based on delusional optimism rather than on a rational weighting of gains, losses and probabilities. They overestimate benefits and underestimate costs. They spin overconfident scenarios of success while overlooking or downplaying the potential for mistakes and miscalculations. Consequently, initiatives are pursued that are unlikely to come in on budget or on time or to deliver the expected returns, or even to be completed. In this overoptimistic stance, they are often aided and abetted by those in the industry.

In a prescient comment on the Lovallo and Kahneman (2003) article, Flyvbjerg (2003) made the point – on which he was later to expand – that Lovallo and Kahneman underrate one source of bias in forecasting, namely the deliberate 'cooking' of forecasts to get ventures started. He termed this the 'Machiavelli factor' (ibid., p. 121).

MACHIAVELLIAN MEGAPROJECTS

Flyvbjerg et al. (2002), Mott MacDonald (2002) and Mackie and Preston (1998) all identify overcommitment of political prestige at an early stage, late changes to project design, failure to engage interest groups and consider external effects, lack of attention to regulatory impacts, and an overemphasis on technical factors for poor megaproject outcomes. Notably, however, Flyvbjerg et al. (2002) explicitly reject the idea that the differences between forecast and actual costs and revenues can be attributed to the innate difficulty of predicting the future. Rather, they look instead to three contributing elements:

1. *Short political tenure.* Politicians involved in advocating projects on the basis of overoptimistic forecasts are often not in office when actual viability can be checked.
2. *Rent-seeking behaviour.* Special-interest groups can promote projects at no cost or risk to themselves.

3. *'Putting on a good spin'.* Contractors are keen to have their proposals
    accepted during tendering, and the penalties for producing overoptimistic
    tenders are often slight.

In effect, project promoters appear to think that a degree of deception and delu-
sion is necessary to get projects started, and they are supported by engineers
with a 'monument complex' and by 'empire-building politicians' in pursuit of
'vanity projects' with access to public funds (Flyvbjerg et al., 2003, pp. 45–8).

Flyvbjerg (2008, p. 136) refers to such deception and misrepresentation as
'the dark side of project development'. This describes his second situational
case, where planners and politicians do not find it important to get forecasts
right and where, in fact, they do not help to clarify and mitigate risk but instead
generate and exacerbate it. Planners are part of the problem, not the solution,
because they are not interested in being accurate and unbiased in forecasting.
Instead, the aim is to get the project off the ground and underway.

Two reasons are advanced for this state of affairs. Planning ought to be open
and communicative, but often it is closed. Desirably, planning would be par-
ticipatory and democratic, but frequently it is used as an instrument to control
and suppress dissent. Planning should be based on rationality, but instead it
is about power (Flyvbjerg, 1998). These circumstances are what Flyvbjerg
(1996) identifies as the 'dark side' of planning.

Forecasting, too, has its dark side. It is in this context that we find Wachs's
(1989) lying planners. They are busy, not with getting forecasts right, but
with getting projects funded and built. Accurate forecasts may not achieve
this objective. Biased forecasts may be the best way to compete for funds and
secure the go-ahead for construction. 'The most effective planner', says Wachs
(1989, p. 477), 'is sometimes the one who can cloak advocacy in the guise of
scientific or technical rationality.' Seemingly technically derived forecasts that
underestimate costs and overestimate benefits, judged on the extent to which
they occur, appears apparently to be a successful formula for gaining project
approval. Forecasting here is just another kind of rent-seeking behaviour. Risk
is not a result of error but of misinformation (Flyvbjerg, 2008).

Flyvbjerg (2005, p. 18) coined the term 'Machiavellian Megaprojects', sug-
gesting that infrastructure megaprojects were the result of the application of a
'Machiavellian formula'. That is, in order to get an infrastructure project built:

(underestimate costs)
+ (overestimate revenues)
+ (undervalue environmental and social impacts)
+ (overvalue wider economic development effects, or spillover effects)
= (win project approval)

A particularly revealing articulation of the 'get things off the ground or nothing will be built' mentality is given in Flyvbjerg (2014, p. 6). Former mayor of San Francisco and former speaker of the California State Assembly, Willie Brown, discussing a large cost overrun on the San Francisco Transbay Terminal megaproject in his *San Francisco Chronicle* column of 28 July 2013, wrote:

> News that the Transbay Terminal is something like $300 million over budget should not come as a shock to anyone. We always knew the initial estimate was way under the real cost, just like we never had a real cost for the [San Francisco] Central Subway or the [San Francisco–Oakland] Bay Bridge or any other massive construction project. So get off it. In the world of civic projects, the first budget is really just a down payment. If people knew the real cost from the start, nothing would ever be approved. The idea is to get going. Start digging a hole and make it so big, there's no alternative to coming up with the money to fill it in. (Ibid., p. 12)

As Flyvbjerg observes, rarely has the tactical use by project advocates of cost underestimation, sunk costs and lock-in to get projects started been expressed by an insider more plainly, if somewhat cynically.

A theoretical justification for the 'nothing would ever get done' position is provided by Hirschman and Sawyer (Flyvbjerg, 2016). Hirschman (1967) made the observation that humans are 'tricked' into doing big projects by their own ignorance. This trickery is seen as positive because, just like humans underestimate the difficulties in doing large-scale projects, they also underestimate their own creativity in dealing with the difficulties. 'The only way in which we can bring our creative sources fully into play is by misjudging the nature of the task, by presenting it to ourselves as more routine, simple, undemanding of genuine creativity than it will turn out to be.' Hirschman dubbed this the 'principle of the Hiding Hand', and it consists of 'some sort of invisible or hidden hand that beneficially hides difficulties for us', where the error of underestimating difficulties is offset by a 'roughly similar' error in underestimating our ability to overcome the difficulties, thus helping to 'accelerate the rate at which "mankind" engages successfully in problem-solving' (ibid., pp. 13–14).

Sawyer (1952), in a study of early industrial infrastructure projects that he dubbed 'in praise of folly', similarly identified what he called 'creative error' in project development as, first, 'miscalculation or sheer ignorance' of the true costs and benefits of projects; and second, such miscalculation being 'crucial to getting an enterprise launched at all'. Sawyer argued that 'creative error' was the key to building a number of large and historically important projects. Although Sawyer's paper predates it, the Sydney Opera House illustrates this point well. Despite a cost overrun of 1400 per cent (the third-highest ever), few regret its iconic status, notwithstanding its recent tag as 'the world's worst example of megaproject planning' (Irvine, 2013).

Flyvbjerg (2014) dismisses the 'Hidden Hand' rationale with the comment, 'The logic is seductive, but precarious' (p. 6), on the grounds of the apparent licence it gives for the 'unfittest' ventures to survive through deception, while other potentially worthwhile projects may not get under way (Flyvbjerg, 2009). Admittedly, however, the 'get things off the ground' view does fall on particularly fertile ground. Flyvbjerg (2012) speaks of the 'four sublimes' of megaproject projects. First, there is the technological dimension, and the kudos that comes from demonstrating what technology can achieve in terms of the tallest building, the longest bridge, the deepest tunnel and so on. Second, there is the political dimension, catering to the monument-building complex. Megaprojects are media magnets, and garner regional, national and even international attention. Third, there is the economic perspective, with an enormous budget to be spread around among consultants, designers, contractors, engineers, architects, financiers, investors, lawyers, developers, and even artists whose art is chosen to grace the inside and outside of the building. Finally, there is the aesthetic viewpoint, and the desire for an iconic structure such as the Eiffel Tower, the Chrysler Building, the Golden Gate Bridge, or the Guggenheim Museum Bilbao.

In such an environment and context, the question may be not so much what planners can do to reduce inaccuracy and risk in forecasting, but what others can do to impose on planners the checks and balances that would stop them producing biased forecasts, act professionally, and not be bullied by politicians and others with vested interests to produce the 'right' answers. Regrettably, the use of consultants and advisers may not always help, for some of their number may be similarly inclined to tell people what they want to hear. The client–consultant relationship is a complex one and the value of their interrelationship depends on both parties being open to the principle of frank and fearless advice. A good adviser helps a client to understand the problem first, and not simply back-solve to a predetermined solution.

ARE PPPS THE ANSWER?

In 2004, Darrin Grimsey and I (Grimsey and Lewis, 2004a) put forward the idea that public private partnerships (PPPs) might be one solution to the apparent 'iron law' of megaprojects, namely over budget, over time, over and over again. As we said, a PPP agenda focuses on clearly defining outputs, and expected outcomes, revolves around a detailed business case and project development phase, puts in place project and contract management plans, and involves market testing at a number of levels. A PPP structure also militates against 'ownership' of the appraisal system by one group and should provide

Table 6.2   *PPP megaprojects, 2001–16, classified by sector*

Sector	PPP megaprojects > US$1 billion
Transport infrastructure	131
Social infrastructure	22
Power	10
Environment	7
Telecommunications	2
Total	172

Note: Includes PPP projects between 1 January 2001 and 25 August 2016.
Source: InfraDeals.

for public scrutiny at a number of points. Further, PPPs add another element, which is a rigorous and robust competitive tendering process.

A key question is whether these features are enough to overcome the decision-making issues with megaprojects outlined above. In 2004, initial evidence on the performance of PPPs and conventional projects appeared promising: Private Finance Initiative (PFI) projects in the 2002 National Audit Office (NAO) census were 76 per cent on time and 78 per cent on budget compared to 30 per cent and 27 per cent respectively for conventional procurement in the 1999 UK government survey. Later evidence was summarized in Grimsey and Lewis (2005b, 2007, 2011). Overall, at least in the past, PPPs have delivered on time and on cost more consistently than traditional procurement.

From the perspective of the present discussion, however, there are two problems with this material. First, the research is somewhat dated. Second, many of the projects may not qualify as megaprojects. Consequently, there appears to be a significant gap in the research to support the question as to whether use of the PPP model currently is delivering similar favourable outcomes on megaprojects. By default, I therefore turn to the anecdotal evidence and consider some examples where PPP has been deployed to deliver megaprojects.

There are now many more PPP megaprojects. According to the Transactions Database of InfraDeals[3] (2016) covering the period from January 2000 to August 2016, around 172 megaproject PPPs (defined as US$1 billion or more) have reached financial close. As summarized in Table 6.2, these mega PPPs involved more than transport (the largest component), including also social infrastructure, power, environment and telecommunications. Unfortunately, no information is given on how the megaprojects have performed. Interestingly, around one-half of these projects are availability-based PPPs, where the purchaser is the government, suggesting that it may have been the application of the PPP model, not the desire to bring in additional private funding, that was an attraction. From knowledge of some of the projects in the database, it can be said that many of them have been delivered successfully on time and on budget (Grimsey and Lewis, 2017). The Victorian Comprehensive Cancer Centre (VCCC) in Melbourne and the Sunshine Coast University Hospital in Queensland are examples in Australia. The A$3.5 billion drought relieving desalination PPP in Victoria got into difficulties in construction, ironically from excessive rain, and eventually it ran over time by 11 months. Other projects also have experienced delay and, in some cases, have resulted in an increase in price to the off-taker (either government or end-users). Nevertheless, the risk allocation appears to have held and the contracts remain and are now delivering services. Finally, a small number have failed and the contract wound up.

Certainly, as megaproject PPPs go, the most spectacular failure of all was that of Metronet in the London Underground project. Richard Little (2011) points out that:

> Many of the problems experienced by megaprojects can be found rooted in poor risk allocation (NRC, 2005) and one of the strongest arguments for the PPP delivery model is that the various project risks are allocated to the party best able to manage them. Who actually bears a risk will be determined by which party is in a better position to control it. (p. 6)

However, this rule cannot stop private firms overreaching themselves and taking on risks that are too large for them to control or manage.

When any megaproject fails, irrespective of whether it is a PPP or not, there are inevitably accusations, blame-throwing and a public furore, and in this instance the House of Commons Committee was unequivocal in advising the Secretary for State on the lessons that it learnt from what is called the 'lamentable state of affairs'.

> Whether or not the Metronet failure was primarily the fault of the particular companies involved, we are inclined to the view that the model itself was flawed and probably inferior to traditional public-sector management ... It is worth remembering that when private companies fail to deliver on large public projects they can walk away – the taxpayer is inevitably forced to pick up the pieces. (House of Commons Transport Committee, 2008, para. 98)

It seems more than likely that this experience had not been forgotten when the PFI scheme was later unwound.

In any case, it is not a question of the PPP model being flawed. PPPs should not be envisaged as a model, sitting in the cupboard ready to pull down and apply. Rather a PPP should be regarded as a step-by-step deliberative process of carefully measuring and evaluating the project risks and putting in place procedures to deal with them. Yet such a process does not prevent sponsors

Table 6.3   *Some failed PPP road infrastructure projects in Australia,
2005–13*

Asset	Daily forecast	Daily actual	Opened	Collapsed
Cross City Tunnel, Sydney	95 000	30 000	2005	2007
Lane Cove Tunnel, Sydney	100 000	55 000	2007	2010
East Link, Melbourne	258 000	134 000	2008	2011
Clem 7, Brisbane	60 000	21 000	2010	2011
Airport Link, Brisbane	130 000	77 000	2012	2013

and other partners, as well as their bankers, from grossly overestimating the demand for the services of the infrastructure.

In Australia, PPP projects that have collapsed include the Cross City Tunnel, Sydney (2007), Lane Cove, Sydney (2010), Airport Link, Brisbane (2013), Clem 7 Tunnel, Brisbane (2011) and East Link, Melbourne (2011) (see Table 6.3). In all cases, the proximate cause was gross overestimates of traffic volumes. Too often the traffic volumes chosen were those that would justify the project proceeding. To some degree the overestimate was a result of drivers' reluctance to pay the tolls (even in some cases when lowered to zero to get people to 'try' the tunnel), although the ready availability of finance in the heady pre-crisis years also played its part in allowing projects to go ahead. As with the subprime crisis of 2007, too much money sloshing around the world led to lax lending decisions and overzealous investors. As a result, hundreds of millions of dollars of private finance were squandered when the project companies that defaulted were later sold at fire-sale prices.

As noted earlier, public procurement is not a one-off or one-shot 'game' in game-theoretic terms, but a repeated one (De Clerk, 2015). Losses must be recovered if the contractors are to stay in business, and future bidding behaviour will not remain invariant in response to such experience. The upshot is that in the aftermath it has been all but impossible to get a privately funded PPP toll road project off the ground in Australia.

One of the criticisms of mega PPPs is that, due to their complexity, there is the potential for opportunism on the part of profit-alert private enterprises involved in PPPs. Yet, there is also potential for opportunism by the public sector. Gloating is one thing, but it does not aid the idea of a partnership between the public sector and the private sector to build infrastructure when the New South Wales premier at the time, Bob Carr (later to become Australia's foreign minister from March 2012 to September 2013), when referring to the Cross City Tunnel project, triumphantly pointed out:

> They owned the road, they carried the risk if they miscalculated … the losses were shifted to the private operators, but that's what the auditor-general told us ought to

happen with these public–private partnerships. We settled on a model so perfect in this respect that the entire cost was borne by private-sector bidders – that's required some modification, but there is nothing dishonest about the model in terms of defending the public interest.

Further, 'We got a new road that threaded traffic under the city, taking thousands of cars a day off the city streets, and the state did not have to put a dollar into it, not a dollar.' To add salt to the wounds, he is reported as making the observation that, during the decade his government was in office, 'the state gained $6 billion in new roads, but the public only contributed $800 million' (Loussikian, 2016, p. 28).[4]

MEGA HOSPITALS

Hospitals are an ideal subject for consideration as megaprojects. They are large, costly to build, costly to fit out and costly to maintain. Moreover, a number have been built in recent years, providing a useful database to study.

In all, 11 mega healthcare PPP projects were examined by Grimsey and Lewis (2017). These were:

- Barts and the London NHS Trust – Hospital Redevelopment, UK (2016)
- Bilkent Integrated Health Campus, Ankara (2017)
- Etlik-Ankara Pilot Hospital, Turkey (2015)
- Halton Healthcare Services – Oakville Hospital P3, Canada (2015)
- Humber River Regional Hospital, Canada (2015)
- McGill University Health Centre – MUHC – Glen Campus, Canada (2015)
- Montreal University Hospital Centre – CHUM, Canada (2016)
- New Karolinska University Hospital, Sweden (2018)
- Royal Adelaide Hospital (RAH), South Australia (2017)
- Sunshine Coast University Hospital (SCUH), Queensland, Australia (2017)
- Victorian Comprehensive Cancer Centre (VCCC) PPP, Australia (2016).

According to the analysis in Grimsey and Lewis (2017), three of the PPP projects appear to have been delivered on time and budget (Halton, Humber, VCCC), one over time (Montreal), two in dispute, with one on time (McGill) and the other over time (RAH), and the remaining five projects are not fully resolved.

In ranking the 11 hospitals, instead of total cost, the cost per hospital bed is a more useful point of comparison. Figure 6.1 provides this analysis and indicates that the Royal Adelaide Hospital (RAH) has the highest cost per hospital bed of the group. At a contracted price of A$1.85 billion, to which had been added A$494 million of state-funded works, making a total cost of A$2.34 billion, it is unquestionably a very expensive building by world stand-

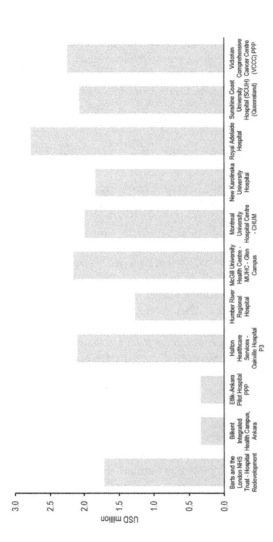

Note: *The capex cost for each hospital has been converted to USD in 2015, allowing for FX movements from financial close and construction escalation costs from construction completion where applicable. The cost per hospital bed is in accordance with the Canadian Union of Public Employees, 'Research Report, P3 Hospitals: The Wrong Direction', April 2011, which found that the North Bay P3 hospital (Ontario) price per bed is just under C$1.5 million ($1430412.17) (https://cupe.ca/sites/cupe/files/cupe_p3_hospital_research_report_-_april_20111.pdf).

Sources: InfraDeals for capex costs and various sources for number of hospital beds. Eurostat, File: EU28 EA19 Countries construction cost annual rates of change 2005–15 – for UK, Turkey and Sweden; Statistics Canada, Construction price indexes (apartment building) – for Canada; Australian Bureau of Statistics, Table 18, Input to the house construction industry, six state capital cities, weighted average and city, index numbers and percentage changes – for Australia. OECD Data, Exchange rates, Total, National currency units/USD, 2000–15.

Figure 6.1 Indicative cost per hospital bed (based on the total capex cost and number of hospital beds per facility)*

ards (Kenny and Booth, 2015; Booth and Hutchinson, 2016). However, some iconic and innovative features are relevant to this comparison:

- The hospital works on a vertical integration system, using lifts rather than long corridors.
- Robots are used. C-3PO-type robots deliver linen and food trolleys, along with some instruments. As the robots move around, they are equipped to recognize people and will 'politely' ask them to move aside.
- The lift system separates the robots' lifts from lifts for the visiting public and also from patients' lifts. 'Hot' lifts are reserved for emergency movements without unnecessary stops.
- There are 40 identical large technical suites (operating theatres, intervention suites and procedure rooms).
- It features 100 per cent overnight single-patient rooms with private ensuites, and there are facilities for visiting families to stay overnight.
- The building is extensively 'green', featuring rainwater and stormwater harvesting, high-efficiency water fittings, a thermal plant, extensive daylight penetration, and sky gardens.

While the RAH has a noticeably higher cost per bed than the other megaprojects, it has some unique features, as noted above, such as 100 per cent single occupancy rooms and robotic logistics. Both of these aspects raise the capital costs, but also have the potential to improve health outcomes and reduce the costs of running the facility (logistics). Also, increased upfront capital cost often generates lower whole-of-life facilities costs and enhanced throughput. This is where the PPP model creates the incentives for the private sector under competition to optimize costs over the life of the infrastructure, and why focusing on one category of total cost (i.e. capital) alone is not an embracing or complete measure of value for money. By the same token, there may be an element of 'gold-plating' involved, which has raised the ire of some taxpayers, although the feedback from patients has been mainly positive.

Nevertheless, it is fair to say that, because of the overall cost and inadequacies at times in the overworked emergency facilities, the RAH had a poor reputation among the general public (a bit of a 'white elephant'). That, fortunately, began to change with the COVID-19 pandemic, and the RAH is now being hailed as 'an example to the world' (Crouch, 2020), as the iconic features came into their own:

- Single-patient rooms minimize infection risk.
- Robots move linen and food with minimal human contact.
- Each patient room can be monitored and the temperature and so on changed from a central point.
- Air conditioning can be set to 'pandemic mode' to isolate selected areas.

- Treatment facilities are vertically stacked for quick access from a rescue helicopter.
- Green spaces and numerous courtyards allow for social distancing.
- Ability to quickly create a separate COVID-testing clinic for up to 200 patients a day.
- No need to install Perspex screens, since there are no shared rooms.

All in all, the RAH is now seen globally as a standout facility.

In conclusion, despite the above-mentioned delays to PPP megaprojects, it is important to appreciate that there are very different consequences when a PPP runs over time, as compared with a conventionally procured project. Under a PPP, the state is compensated for the delay and does not start paying for the new facility until it is commissioned. In effect, no money leaves the Treasury until that happens. By contrast, things are quite different under a traditional contract where the government would have paid for the project in stage payments, putting it in a potentially weaker position. In the case of the RAH, the outcome of the delay was unclear for some time. Yet, the contract remained in place until the hospital was eventually commissioned. All of this meant that the Government of South Australia did not make any payments for the use of the facility until the hospital was finally commissioned and in this way the risk transfer for on-time delivery of the project held up.

These examples, being anecdotal, do not establish whether PPPs are, or are not, suitable for delivery of megaprojects, any more than they would in the case of any other procurement approach. What does seem clear is that PPPs can work, but are not suitable for all projects. Developing a careful and rigorous procurement strategy is essential if any project, and especially a megaproject, is to be successfully delivered. It is the combination of objectives, characteristics, risks and value drivers inherent in the project that must dictate the most suitable procurement model for its delivery, rather than some blind faith in a delivery model to fix problems for the project sponsor.

NOTES

1. The major and notable exception is the Channel Tunnel.
2. Situations of uncertainty can be distinguished sharply from those of risk despite the fact that in both instances the actual future outcome is not predictable with certainty. For example, 'A *risky* situation is one in which the probability distribution of outcomes is known; an *uncertain* situation is one in which even this information is totally lacking' (Marglin, 1967, p. 71). In effect, risk is concerned with known probabilities, uncertainty with 'unknown unknowns'. Uncertainty is considered in Grimsey and Lewis (2004a, 2017) and the analysis is not repeated here.
3. https://www.opendemocracy.net/ournhs/john-lister/bart%E2%80%99s-flagship -hits-rocks-of-pfi.

4.   Given Mr Carr's favourable experience as a procurer of PPPs, it is perhaps not surprising that in the aftermath of the 2020 US election he criticized Donald Trump when President for not assembling a quality infrastructure package deploying public private partnerships! (Carr, 2020).

7.   Where to now for PPPs?

THE ADVISERS

From the viewpoint of many of those opposed to public private partnerships (PPPs), those accounting and other firms providing financial advisory services to the infrastructure industry are regarded with suspicion, and seen as flagbearers of a PPP-centric agenda, encouraging public sector procurers to undertake PPPs vis-à-vis conventional procurement methods. Of course, such a charge if true would constitute a severe breach of a professional adviser–client relationship. As well, it should be recalled that PPPs represent 10 per cent or less of infrastructure procurement, with the vast bulk of the remaining projects undertaken by traditional methods. Further, a number of projects that were investigated as to their viability as PPPs have instead been judged by the advisers as being more suited to conventional procurement, and have progressed through to completion on that basis. Invariably, the documentation put out by the advisory bodies emphasizes choosing the procurement approach that is appropriate for the project and its objectives.

Two recent reports have been released by advisers in Australia, namely *Reimagining Public Private Partnerships* (PWC, 2017) and *Where to Now for the PPP Model?* (EY, 2020). From the two reports, some inkling can be gained of what the advisers are thinking, and how they view the situation, and prospects, in the PPP market. These two reports can be supplemented by a new study, titled *Measuring the Value and Service Outcomes of Social Infrastructure PPPs in Australia and New Zealand*, commissioned from the University of Melbourne by the industry group Infrastructure Partnerships Australia of Social Infrastructure PPPs (IPA, 2020). It is that report, and social infrastructure PPPs in particular, that is first considered.

SOCIAL INFRASTRUCTURE

PPPs have proven to be popular for social infrastructure projects in Australia, with 39 projects completed between 1998 and 2020. There is a perception that the PPP model is well suited (even 'ideal') for social infrastructure such as hospitals, schools, even prisons. It would seem that the 'sweet spot' is for medium-sized projects between $100 million to $2 billion, in terms of Australian dollars.

Judging from the IPA study, there appears to be considerable satisfaction with the PPPs concerned, at least among the service providers. Service providers are defined in the report as those utilizing the PPP facility to deliver services to their client community members. Examples are school principals, doctors, wardens, and administrative or management staff, employed either in the public sector or through the PPP consortium. They were surveyed in the study to determine whether mature PPP social infrastructure projects met the service delivery outcomes expected by users of the facility. Specifically, the survey sought to assess whether the increases in service benefits promised by the proponents of the PPP model to service providers, and hence in turn their client community, had been achieved.

Results of the survey are as follows:

- It was found that PPP projects do deliver on the services as promised by governments and government departments and public bodies in media releases, community information documents and public meetings.
- All service providers reported that the PPP projects investigated opened for service to the community on time, and that since that time they have performed better than facilities run under the traditional model.
- An overwhelming preference was found among service providers for working within a PPP facility over that of a traditional government-owned and operated facility.
- Service providers were of a mind that the PPP projects were delivering value for money (VfM), while at the same time identifying opportunities for the evolution and continued improvement in the PPP model.
- The researchers' analysis of project documentation appeared to show that the VfM originally evaluated by government as a part of the tender process was maintained throughout the operating phase of the PPP agreement, with no evidence of risk transfer back to government.
- Service providers expressed a strong appreciation of the quality of services provided by the Facility Management (FM) operator in a PPP facility. Satisfaction levels with service quality was strongly influenced by the experience level and relationship between service providers, contract managers and FM operators.
- All service providers agreed that the PPP model provided similar flexibility provisions to traditional procurement models.

One qualification to the results comes from the finding that service providers are poorly informed about the difference between PPP and traditionally procured facilities, so restricting their effectiveness in the PPP facility.

Nevertheless, the researchers conclude that governments should continue to consider and use the PPP model for social infrastructure service delivery as a way of bringing greater benefits to service providers and users, and better value for taxpayers.

THE ADVISERS' REPORTS

Both reports have a starting point that, for suitable projects, PPPs have the potential to deliver better value for money than alternative delivery approaches. This outcome can be achieved in a variety of ways, usually by a combination of the infrastructure solution producing superior outcomes, less risk for government and lower whole-of-life cost. However, such a result is incumbent on selecting an appropriate project and carefully planning and managing the process.

Merits of PPPs

In this context, the PPP approach is seen to have the following merits:

- *Delivery.* PPPs enjoy a good reputation for achieving on-time and within-budget delivery.
- *Certainty.* When entered into, PPPs provide contractual and budget certainty for the entire transaction over the life of the project. For other procurement models there are separate deals made for design, construction, operation and maintenance, at prices determined at the time and with the full cost only known at the end. With the PPP, all necessary contracts are signed before the government becomes bound by the portmanteau contract.
- *Scoping.* Project scoping is improved. The long-term nature of PPP contracts forces government procurers to think carefully about the service outcomes that are to be sought, and what the alternatives are. As a consequence, the documents are more likely to be output-focused.
- *Risk assessment.* For broadly similar reasons, the extent of risk assessment by government bodies when entering into a PPP likely far exceeds that for traditional procurement. In theory, the same degree of scoping and risk assessment could be applied to conventional procurement, but the longer time frame of PPPs and the larger expenditure sharpens the government's focus.
- *Innovation.* Due to the output and performance focus of PPP contracting, there is a greater incentive for the private sector bodies to come up with solutions that generate the specified service level at lower whole-of-life costings. Again, there is no reason why innovative solutions cannot be sought under a traditional procurement bidding process. Whether it is

sensible to expect innovation under a PPP or via traditional arrangement is another question. Innovation is much less safe than sticking to tried and tested methods for projects. Inevitably, then, innovation is risky and, if desired, may be better sought under a risk-sharing procurement approach, such as alliancing.[1]

- *Private finance.* The advisers attribute much of the certainty on the cost and time outcomes of PPPs to the involvement of private investors and debt financiers under limited recourse finance. However, it must be said that the financiers have not always been as hard-nosed as they were meant to be, swinging between providing too much finance on easy terms in the upswing and then pulling in their horns and rationing credit on much harsher terms during the downswing. Such behaviour seems to be a perennial problem.[2]

- *Upfront budget.* The special purpose vehicle (SPV) formed for the PPP is required to deliver maintenance and other services to a specified standard throughout the term of the contract. In this way, the PPP model forces the PPP sponsors and investors to plan ahead and budget upfront for the needed maintenance.

- *Risk transfer.* Under conventional procurement policies, risk taken on by government in owning and operating infrastructure typically carries substantial, and often undervalued, cost. One of the main aims when the public procurer opts to choose a PPP project is to transfer risk from the government to the private sector. What risks are transferred, and to whom, is determined on a project-by-project basis, using a risk matrix of the type outlined by Grimsey and Lewis (2002) as a general organizing framework. Transferring some of the risk to a private party which can manage it at less cost can reduce the overall cost to government, although it is not cost-effective to transfer all risks. A PPP seeks to achieve the 'best' allocation.

Consequently, when prepared and used wisely, a risk matrix can be a useful tool to both government practitioners and the private sector. Optimal risk allocation aims to minimize both the chances of project risks materializing and the repercussions if they do. It has two elements: (1) optimal risk management and the impetus to achieve it; and (2) value for money. The first of these is based on the view that the party best able to control a risk should be allocated that risk. The second element – value for money – is related to the first, in that the party best able to manage a risk should also be able to manage it at least cost.

On practical grounds, the government must identify, on a project-by-project basis, the risks that it will take on before it puts the project to the market. Generally speaking, those risks assumed by government are likely to include factors such as the risk of legislation or of a policy change discriminating against the project, the risk of government wishing to change (e.g. increase) the service standards or volumes, some elements of antiquities or indigenous title risk and some elements of pre-existing latent defect and contamination risk. Table 7.1 illustrates how an allocation might work out in practice. Prison PPPs have not been greatly discussed so far, and the example given is that of a PPP for a privately operated prison project under the 'serviced infrastructure' model.[3]

That is all fairly standard fare. However, as the PricewaterhouseCoopers (PWC, 2017) report pointed out, it is worth noting that the government entity achieves additional risk transfer under a PPP that is not achieved under more traditional procurement models. First, in the case of user-charge PPPs, demand risk is typically transferred to the SPV and its equity investors and debt financiers. Second, under the PPP model, the private finance provided by the SPV's equity investors and debt financiers provides government with a buffer against the risks of contractor insolvency, and also because the equity investors and debt financiers will generally invest additional resources in solving problems caused by contractor default or insolvency if failing to do so would reduce the value of their investment or loan. Third, the imposition of the SPV between the government and the

Table 7.1   *Risk allocation in a PPP prison project*

Government risks	Private sector risks	Shared risks
Site approvals	Site conditions	Technology
Specifications/cell design functionality	Contractor design fault	Custodial best design
	Cost overrun	*Force majeure*
Contractual land use rights	Construction delay	
Change to licence conditions	Building maintenance/service cost overrun	
Government delays, e.g. granting approvals	Shortfall in quality	
Demand risk	Performance-availability of accommodation at required standards	
Political/sovereign risks	Prisoner mix within bands, i.e. flexibility to respond to change	
Discriminatory change in law	Changes in general taxes and tariffs	
	Changes in interest rates	
	Non-discriminatory change in law	
	Environmental risks	

Source: Grimsey and Lewis (2004b), Table 7.2.

contractors on a PPP can have the practical effect of shielding the government from claims made by the contractors for extra time and/or extra money. Under a PPP contract, such claims by contractors must be brought against the SPV in the first instance. It will then be a matter for the SPV to decide whether or not the claim should be passed upstream to the government. Finally, on most PPPs, there are no progress payments made that are to be recovered, as the government agency is not obliged to make any payments until construction is completed and service provision commences.

Problems of PPPs

The advisers' reports consider a number of matters that have already been covered in earlier chapters, such as the inflexibility of PPPs and refinancing gains ('excessive profits' and 'windfall gains'). Therefore, the discussion here will continue on with a number of risk transfer aspects highlighted in the two reports.

• *Failed (insolvent) projects.* Very few service-payment PPPs in Australia have resulted in an insolvency. Most of the 'failed PPPs' in Australia have been user-charge PPPs, where the revenue generated by the project was well below that forecast by the consortium's investors, leading to the insolvency of the SPV.

But does the insolvency of the SPV really mean that the PPP has failed? Consider, for example, the case of the Cross City Tunnel, which is one of the failed toll roads. It runs under Sydney's Central Business District (CBD), connecting the eastern side to the western side. The capital expenditure cost of the project was A$680 million (2002). The road reached financial close in 2002 and opened to traffic in 2005 after being delivered on time and on budget. It is an engineering triumph, consisting of two (east and west) 2.1 km tunnels, along with a third service tunnel, and was procured under a 33-year concession period. The objective of the PPP, to a considerable extent realized, was to reduce traffic congestion, improve the environmental amenity in Sydney's CBD and improve east to west traffic flows in the CBD. Nevertheless, the PPP has been criticized and labelled as a failure by local media and commentators, largely due to improper allocation of risk, inaccurate traffic forecasting and negative consumer response to changed traffic conditions and road closures, which were perceived by the public as attempts to force traffic onto the toll road. The operating company went into receivership less than two years after commencing operations.

The failure of the PPP resulted in recriminations, public anger and a questioning of the PPP model for this project. The road has since been bought by Transurban Group and traffic revenues have remained stable.

While the project failed to achieve the revenue forecasts, the consequences of this risk were borne as intended, that is, first by the equity investors and then by the lenders. From their perspectives, the project failed. Yet, the objectives of the state government and also the SPV's contractors were achieved, and from their perspective the project can be considered as a success. Moreover, much as it may grate the private entities involved, the government did not have to bail out the project via additional government funding, while a significant piece of infrastructure was delivered at a cost to taxpayers much less than would have been the case had the government procured it under a publicly funded delivery model.

Not that the government escaped scot-free, because the downside for the government was that equity investors and debt financiers quickly lost their appetite for demand risk on greenfield transport projects. This forced the public sector to use contractual delivery models under which the government itself bears much more demand risk.

- *Asset recycling.* As the situation then stood, governments wanted to institute greenfield transport projects, but private firms have backed away from taking on the inherent risks. On this interpretation, it would seem that if governments are to implement infrastructure projects, they have themselves to take on the role of developer, most certainly bearing risk on the revenue side, and perhaps partially as well on the construction side. At the same time, there seems to be no shortage of investors willing to buy 'mature' ('brownfield') infrastructure assets. This juxtaposition underpins the idea of 'asset recycling'.

Asset (or capital) recycling enables governments to fund higher-risk projects by selling off assets once they have reached the stage at which risks are lower (Ergas, 2014). In a way, the build, own, operate, transfer (BOOT) model PPP is turned on its head. Now it is the government that has to build, own and operate infrastructure before transferring it to the private sector (Gelber, 2014). A relatively common method used is the government buys, tolls then sells (GBTS) model. Private sector contractors are engaged to design, build and maintain a road, and to install tolling equipment, under public-funded contracts. Government retains the tolls collected during the ramp-up period as the project builds some actual traffic history. Once actual traffic levels have been established, the public sector sells the right to levy and collect future tolls to the private sector. With this approach, the government bears traffic risk during the ramp-up period, and the private sector bears traffic risk after ramp up, when the risk is considerably reduced.

Is asset recycling perhaps a temporary response to changed conditions in which investors seemingly have a greatly reduced appetite for greenfield transport projects, or is it something more? Levitt and Eriksson (2019,

p. 116) argue that 'the asset recycling mechanism relies on a new vision of the role of government as an efficient, effective and risk-taking investor in infrastructure'. They envisage 'a future model for infrastructure service delivery', in which the government either:

1. Finances and develops an asset itself and sells the up-and-running 'brownfield' asset to an operator, with the proceeds placed into an infrastructure asset recycling fund, or
2. Issues a concession to a private concessionaire for the delivery of infrastructure service for an extended period, with the private entity responsible for financing, designing, constructing, operating, and maintaining the infrastructure service. (Ibid., p. 119)

In the same volume, Nowacki (2019) takes a more measured approach. She begins by pointing out that infrastructure asset recycling consists of two legs: selling or leasing existing assets, and reinvesting the proceeds into new infrastructure assets. She then goes on:

With asset recycling, the government obtains funds when leasing an asset, but commits to giving away user fees or giving availability payments to the leaseholder. On its balance sheet, it has also exchanged capital for cash. Theoretically, the government did not create value. In practice, it can make a profit if the bid value is higher than the present value of the future cash flows it would have received from owning and operating the asset. In that case, the value creation is highly dependent on the procurement process, and the ability of the government to attract multiple investors to compete in the bid and package the deal so that, from their point of view, the money it gets is superior to the net present value (NPV) of future cash flows. (Ibid., p. 261)

Her conclusion is:

In summary, asset recycling makes the government give up future cash flows from existing projects to fund the construction of new projects. However operation and maintenance costs still need to be covered by other sources of funds, taxes or user fees; and ideally construction costs would also be recouped through these funding sources if the government does not want to lose capital. (Ibid., p. 253)
[It] is therefore not strictly a funding mechanism, as the government gains access to new capital only when it makes a profit on a transaction. Thinking of it as a financing mechanism might be closer, but comparing it to other financing mechanisms does not do justice to the freedom it gives to government, and the potential other benefits brought by privatizing selected projects. (Ibid., p. 253)

- *Illusory risk transfer.* Critics of PPPs contend that the risk transfer under a PPP is illusory because ultimately the government is the risk bearer of last resort. Thus, in some Australian PPPs the government has felt the need to either take control of the project or provide additional financial support to a project because the private sector had not been able to manage the risks that it had accepted. Mostly, these circumstances were triggered by a failure by the private entities to provide adequate service levels in hospital PPPs. In the case of the Cross City Tunnel and some other transport PPPs, matters were resolved without the governments needing to inject financial support.

For the future, however, as the focus of PPPs shifts from social infrastructure to megaprojects designed to reduce congestion, improve transport safety, stimulate economic growth and productivity, lower environmental impacts and so on, there is a worry that the PPP model may be found wanting – a major concern of the Ernst & Young (EY) report, for instance. Historical risk allocations, for example those adopted for social infrastructure projects, need to be reassessed when dealing with transport megaprojects. When projects involve extensive tunnelling and geophysical risks, as in the Melbourne Underground availability-based PPP project currently underway, the question becomes not just who is best placed to manage the risks, but who can afford to take on these risks! More genuine collaboration may be needed, and the 'partnership' element of PPPs brought to the fore.

NOTES

1. Because this volume is about PPPs, other procurement models such as alliancing have not featured prominently. An alliance contract is a 'relationship contract', in effect a 'true' partnership that essentially turns a project into a joint venture. Under this model, two or more entities agree to undertake the work in cooperation, taking decisions jointly, and the aim is to align the participants' objectives to maximize performance, proactively manage risk, reduce time and cost, and achieve innovative solutions. It is characterized by:
   - *Collective assumption of all risk:* all participants jointly assume and manage every risk relevant to the success of the project.
   - *No dispute:* a 'no fault, no blame' regime enables the alliance leadership team to ensure tensions are resolved among participants, and excludes the ability to issue legal proceedings against each other, except in the case of wilful default.
   - *The compensation framework:* this provides for direct cost reimbursement on an open book basis, a fee to contribute to the participants' profit and corporate overhead, and a gain share/pain share (or risk/reward) regime where cost savings and cost overruns are shared equitably among participants.
   - *Good faith:* all participants are required to act in good faith and with integrity to make unanimous, best-for-project decisions.
   Creating alliances may be suitable where the project is complex and involves unpredictable risks, which if transferred to the private sector using traditional delivery methods would be cost prohibitive, and there is a compressed delivery

programme which requires a flexible approach to incorporate economic, political or stakeholder considerations. For example, three of the six major desalination plants in Australia were built under alliance contracts when there was a desire to build them quickly. Of the other three plants, one was a design and construct, and the other two were PPPs, one a design, build, operate, maintain (DBOM), the other a design, build, finance, operate, maintain (DBFOM) (Grimsey and Lewis, 2017).

2.   See, for example, my own catalogue of banks' behaviour in the 1980s (Lewis, 1994), in the Asian financial crisis (Bentick and Lewis, 2004) and in the global financial crisis of 2008 (Lewis, 2010, 2011).

3.   Under this model, prison services are divided into three categories:

   •   Core services under public sector control and excluded from the contract, that is, billets (cleaning/laundry/catering), industries and custodial operations.
   •   Services provided by a private sector partner (infrastructure plus ancillary services), that is, accommodation, security systems, estate management, transport and information systems management.
   •   Those services with the potential for private sector provision but excluded from the contract at the outset, namely medical, education, works and vocational training.

   Under the contract term of up to 40 years, the public sector operator is responsible for specifying in output terms the custodial aspects of the design of the facilities, that is, functional content/adjacencies, but without extending to engineering and construction responsibility for any aspect. Other than this, the SPV is responsible for all aspects of the design and the construction works as a whole, including structural integrity, circulation space, foundations, air conditioning and so on, with payments linked directly to performance and other criteria.

8. Conclusions

THE BOOK SO FAR

Chapter 1 set the scene in two ways. First, it introduced the concept of bundling in construction generally, and specifically in what Broadbent and Laughlin (2003) call the Long-Term Infrastructure Contract (LTIC) type public private partnership (PPP). Bundling can be regarded as the defining characteristic of a PPP. Second, the chapter considered powerful criticisms of PPPs from three sources. One, which has the potential to turn out to be a dramatic fall from grace for PPPs, comes from the UK Treasury, which has decided that no new contracts for PFI and PF2 (the latest incarnations of PPPs) would be signed. The other two sources are the Civil Society Organization (CSO) report of ten case studies of PPPs across the world and 12 audits by the European Court of Auditors. In all cases, PPPs were found wanting. Together, the combined weight of the three provides a compelling reason for rethinking the PPP model.

PPPs have their own inner logic in terms of incentive compatibility, whole-of-life costings and risk transfer, but from where did the idea come? This was the topic of Chapter 2, which began with the intellectual structure of research into PPPs and outlined and reviewed the five most cited works in the literature. PPPs formed part of a changed environment and different agenda for public services, which included contracting out and privatization, but the chapter argued that PPPs are neither of these. Instead, the design, build, finance, operate (DBFO) model developed for British highways allied with project finance techniques provided the underpinning for the PPP model. It is easy to overlook that at that time there was considerable disappointment with conventional procurement outcomes, which served to propel the experimentation with PPPs.

Economic theory suggests that any performance differences relative to traditional procurement methods can be attributed to those characteristics of PPPs which differentiate them from conventional procurement. Chapter 3 began by exploring these differences and how they might, at least in theory, bring about superior performance outcomes for PPPs because of the distinctive incentive structures introduced into the procurement process. Then the chapter considered seven myths about the costs and benefits of PPPs, before going on to examine seven misconceptions as to what PPPs can and cannot do. These analyses were followed by a number of controversies that commonly feature in criticisms of PPPs. Finally, the chapter ended by examining what may be seen as the Achilles heel of PPPs, which is their complexity, although it is shown that there are in fact many dimensions to complexity.

Chapter 4 began with what readers may have already discerned is my bugbear with the 'lower cost of government borrowing' position that appears to have killed off the Private Finance Initiative (PFI) in the UK, a decision that may reverberate around the global PPP market. While I may argue until I am blue in the face, the reality is that government can access cheaper finance than private entities (albeit by assuming more risk), and esoteric economic views about how wrong-headed this is are unlikely to carry much weight in public policy circles. Accordingly, the chapter looked at the alternatives, including, with finance removed, a design, build, operate, maintain (DBOM) PPP model, and the chapter also assessed whether there might be non-financial benefits from the PPP model worth countenancing as a counterweight to the financial case.

Given the questions surrounding the PPP approach to procuring infrastructure, what factors would motivate a government to choose to go down the PPP route? The European PPP Expertise Centre put this question to public authorities and stakeholders involved in implementing PPPs, and the answers received were outlined in Chapter 5. Altogether, 15 principal motivations were identified. In the same report, the public authorities were questioned about the main challenges facing them when implementing PPPs. Thirteen challenges were revealed in their responses, and these were discussed in the chapter.

PPPs have been employed extensively on megaprojects, which were the topic of Chapter 6. Megaprojects pose special problems in decision-making and implementation. A listing of many of the factors discussed in the chapter makes the point: appraisal optimism, optimism bias, inside and outside views of forecasting, the planning fallacy, the sunk-cost fallacy, reference class forecasting, overconfidence, belief perseverance, cognitive dissonance, confirmation bias, groupthink, the Machiavelli factor, rent-seeking, 'putting on a good spin', 'get things off the ground or nothing will be done', 'principle of the Hiding Hand', 'the four sublimes of megaprojects'. The chapter ends with an examination of some PPP megaprojects and the issues raised, along with a comparative study of 11 mega healthcare PPP projects.

Finally, Chapter 7 examined some recent reports on PPPs in Australia. It must be admitted that from the perspective of many of those opposed to PPPs, the accounting and other consulting firms advising governments on public procurement are regarded with suspicion as being flagbearers for PPPs. Nevertheless, this chapter looked at three recent reports, including two from advisory firms, to gain some idea of what the advisers are presently thinking about the PPP market and the issues it faces. The reports do see merits remaining in the PPP approach to public procurement, but they also warn of considerable problems ahead, most notably as the focus of PPPs shifts from social to economic infrastructure, where the risks appear to be much greater and less tractable.

SOME CONCLUDING OBSERVATIONS

Value for money (VfM) has to be a major priority for any government investing in public infrastructure. However, the question as to whether PPPs are in fact delivering value remains an open one. Unfortunately, retrospective evaluation of projects is not rigorously undertaken by government procuring authorities. The UK's National Audit Office (NAO) provides some of the best analysis on the performance of projects, but even it has yet to study comprehensively the performance of PPP projects that are at, or nearing, the end of their contract term, given that whole-of-life is a major attraction of the PPP model.

On this point, it must be said, the academic literature does little better. It has tended to focus on comparative studies on the performance of the construction stage of the PPP as compared to other traditional models. These studies are limited by the commercial-in-confidence nature of government capital infra-structure procurement. Also, it is difficult to ascertain whether it is the model that has failed to deliver or whether it is simply caused by people failing in execution, irrespective of the model. Nevertheless, overall the impression that PPPs deliver on time and on budget does seem to hold up, especially when it is taken into account that many of the costs associated with over-time, over-budget outcomes are not borne by the public procurers but fall upon the contractors.

Difficulties abound when making such performance comparisons. One of the most recent PPP versus conventional procurement studies was published under the auspices of the Organisation for Economic Co-operation and Development (OECD) in 2016. On the face of it, the evidence and assessment provided in this study (Makovšek and Veryard, 2016) appears to be at best inconclusive, at worst unfavourable to PPPs. There are, however, several issues with this study that appear at odds with these conclusions, as Darrin Grimsey and I pointed out (Grimsey and Lewis, 2017).

First, their finding (based on the UK) that PPP hospitals are of no greater quality than those built under traditional procurement is indeed largely correct. But this is not necessarily because the PPP has failed in comparison to traditional procurement. In most hospital PPPs the government, via the National Health Service (NHS) Trust, is the tenant and operates the hospitals and therefore specifies the quality of finishes. It deliberately does so because it does not want gold-plated facilities, and also wants all of its new hospitals to be to a similar standard to its estate, which includes traditionally built hospitals. Such behaviour does limit the effectiveness of the PPP approach in terms of both quality of finish and innovation – the latter being one potential merit of a PPP.

Second, the OECD study by Makovšek and Veryard (2016) cites the roads sector, where the authors say that the capital costs of private roads are substantially higher than those for public procurement. As before, the numbers behind this finding are very likely correct, but again not necessarily for the reason suggested, which was that using the private sector is more expensive than public procurement. This is especially true of motorways, which form the bulk of privately operated PPP roads. Generally, the more that is spent up front, the less is required downstream for maintenance and asset replacement (e.g. concreted roads need much less maintenance than paved roads). This trade-off is a very significant factor for motorways, because these roads carry heavy vehicles that do more than ten times the damage to the surface as compared to cars. Invariably, as should be the case, in a PPP the private sector takes a long-term view and typically tends to invest much more up front, a decision that dramatically reduces the amount needed on both maintenance and life-cycle costs.

A major problem with publicly delivered roads is that they get often get caught up in the political budgeting cycle. Governments are often under pressure to develop more roads, and generally not to use tolls (user pays) to fund (or at least fully fund) these investments. There is thus a great incentive to reduce costs by reducing the quality and durability of the initial construction, and to shift expenditures downstream, perhaps to be dealt with by future governments. Such is the moral hazard of the political process. Private road operators cannot do this, and not only because they know it makes long-term economic sense to build to a higher life-cycle standard. It is also because these projects carry very high performance standards, with financial penalties if they do not perform to requirements. This creates incentives for the private road operators to avoid closing down roads except at strictly scheduled times for maintenance. As a consequence, this means that, typically, the private sector builds to a high quality to mitigate the risk of penalties, keeping the roads open and free from roadworks in order to achieve whole-of-life savings. By contrast, public roads authorities do not have these same performance standards and freely close down lanes for maintenance without penalty. The net result of traditional procurement is a likely higher overall net present cost over the life of the asset, and certainly greater congestion and likely inconvenience to roads users having to go through more contraflows or road blockages (contraflows being a largely British invention which my home state of South Australia regrettably does not use enough).

In summary, the question as to whether the PPP model is delivering superior outcomes on projects cannot be solved by comparative studies involving alternative procurement models. Despite Darrin Grimsey's and my previous work along these lines (Grimsey and Lewis, 2005b, 2007, 2009), it is a false trail. The many procurement models that have been developed have different factors determining their value and merits. Each is appropriate under different circumstances, and VfM is delivered essentially by two things only:

1. The selection of the right procurement model for the project. Every procurement model has its place in the broad frame of things. Each is a valid alternative, and it is a question of matching the characteristics of the project, the specific risks, and the capacity and capability of both the market and the public sector procuring agency. Effectively, while there may be a best procurement model for each project, it is not the only one, and this is one reason why a strict comparison between models to the detriment of one or another is not necessarily a good way to proceed.
2. The recognition that models do not deliver projects, people do. The capacity and capability of the teams in both the public and the private sector is crucial for successful delivery of a project. And the same holds for project selection. Where either the capacity or capability of project management is lacking, then inevitably mistakes are made and value may be diminished. Not only are the skills of the transacting or procurement teams required, but also contract managers must forge long-term working (i.e. true partnership) relationships over the life of a PPP contract if the project is to be successful.

While the PPP model remains controversial, it is no better or worse than any other procurement model, including the traditional forms. All models have their place in best-practice public procurement. It is simply a question of choosing the right model for the project and, importantly, assembling an appropriately skilled workforce to deliver it. For this reason, a comparative study cannot establish that PPPs, or for that matter any other model, can actually deliver better VfM than other alternative models. VfM can therefore only be suggested by retrospective evaluation of performance on an individual project-by-project basis. Moreover, it is the case that people matter to a degree that is neglected in the theoretical literature. The preferred focus ought instead to be on whether the right procurement model is selected and whether the transaction and contract management teams are well chosen and are actually left to do a good job.

A PREFERRED APPROACH

Reiterating what was said above, all procurement models have their distinctive features and have their place. It is a matter of choosing the best one for the job. However, making that choice is not sufficient in itself. Procurement models do not make mistakes; people do. Specification and planning are crucial, as is selecting a good group of contractors to execute the project. In the case of complex PPP megaprojects, for example, the number of participants and specialized skills drawn upon would be as long as the list of credits for a Hollywood movie. They need to be chosen and directed and coordinated. Adopting a model – however appropriate it seems – cannot rescue a poorly conceived, planned and designed project. Nonetheless, a procurement model can prompt the right questions to be asked, put protections in place, and clarify who is responsible for what.

PPPs can bring benefits in these respects. However, the description of 'partnership' remains somewhat of a misnomer. They are not really partnerships in the same way that alliance contracts are. Rather, they are more partnerships in a legal sense, in that PPPs embody strong legal safeguards for the two main parties involved (government and the private special purpose vehicle) and put matters on a firm contractual footing. Because PPPs embrace whole-of-life contracting (design, construction, operation and maintenance) they are necessarily extremely complex and need the right team to be assembled. In this sense, as in most complex things, there is more to go wrong, initially in design and construction, and then later in reaching a reliable determination as to whether the contractor has delivered what was specified to a suitable standard of safety and performance, a judgement which is needed before payments from governments to the contractors can begin.

Since, at least in many eyes, PPPs are the most problematical of the procurement models, Grimsey and Lewis (2017) thought it useful to summarize what has been learnt about their suitability for infrastructure applications:

- PPPs are likely to be most successful in the case of 'greenfield' projects that involve the construction and operation of new infrastructure.
- Conversely, PPPs seem less suited to 'brownfield' infrastructure projects, particularly where the existing infrastructure facilities need to remain fully operational during construction, with difficult access.
- While PPPs have risk transfer at their core, the model is probably not ideal in situations where a project involves excessive amounts of risk that may translate into uncertainty (unknown unknowns) that is less easily dealt with than risk.
- As PPPs rely on risk transfer and a strict underlying contract, they are more readily adaptable to projects where the uncertainties and unknowns are minimized either through well-specified outputs or the existence of reliable data and documentation. That is very hard to achieve where there are existing aged assets, as was proven with the Jubilee Line extension on the London Underground, undoubtedly the worst example of a PPP project.

- When projects are delivered over time, an unfortunate consequence is that the benefits of the infrastructure to the communities and citizens waiting to use the facilities are also delayed. Under PPP contracts, the financial consequences of delay is a risk largely transferred to the private sector, which does not receive any payments for the infrastructure until it reaches commercial acceptance. Those PPP projects that have experienced delay obviously have failed to achieve on-time delivery, but most often the cost of this delay finishes up being carried by the private sector.

In general, although by no means universally the case, PPPs have a sound record of avoiding cost overruns and delays, particularly for social infrastructure. While PPPs are not to be preferred for all projects, and constitute only a small proportion of infrastructure constructed, they have undoubtedly informed other procurement approaches by having shown that with the right incentives in place, it is possible for much infrastructure to be delivered on time and on budget, and with the sought after outcomes for the public. In these ways, a richer menu of procurement options is the consequence and, when combined with people skills, excellence in design and good processes, the result can be infrastructure that meets the needs of society at a reasonable cost.

References

Aaltonen, K. and J. Kujala (2010), 'A Project Lifecycle Perspective on Stakeholder Influence Strategies in Global Projects', *Scandinavian Journal of Management*, **26** (4), 381–97.

Altshuler, A. and D. Luberoff (2003), *Mega-Projects: The Changing Politics of Urban Investment*, Washington, DC: Brookings Institution Press.

Argy, F., M. Lindfield, B. Stimson and P. Hollingsworth (1999), 'Infrastructure and Economic Development', CEDA Information Paper No 60, Committee for Economic Development of Australia, Melbourne.

Arkes, H.R. and C. Blumer (1985), 'The Psychology of Sunk Cost', *Organizational Behavior and Human Decision Processes*, **35**, 124–40.

Arrow, K.J. and R.C. Lind (1970), 'Uncertainty and the Evaluation of Public Investment Decisions', *American Economic Review*, **60**, 364–78.

Atkinson, R. (1999), 'Discourses of Partnership and Empowerment in Contemporary British Urban Regeneration', *Urban Studies*, **36**, 59–72.

Bailey, N. (1994), 'Towards a Research Agenda for Public-Private Partnerships in the 1990s', *Local Economy*, **8**, 292–306.

Barberis, N. and R. Thaler (2003), 'A Survey of Behavioural Finance', in G.M. Constantinides, M. Harris and R. Stulz (eds), *Handbook of the Economics of Finance*, Amsterdam: Elsevier, 1051–121.

Barnekov, T., R. Boyle and D. Rich (1989), *Privatism and Urban Policy in Britain and the United States*, Oxford: Oxford University Press.

Batley, R. (1996), 'Public–Private Relationships and Performance in Service Provision', *Urban Studies*, **33** (4–5), 723–51.

Bazelon, Coleman and Kent Smetters (1999), 'Discounting inside the Washington DC Beltway', *Journal of Economic Perspectives*, **13**, 213–28.

Beauregard, R.A. (1998), 'Public-Private Partnerships as Historical Chameleons: The Case of the United States', in J. Pierre (ed.), *Partnerships in Urban Governance: European and American Experience*, New York: St. Martin's Press.

Bénabou, R. (2013), 'Groupthink: Collective Delusions in Organizations and Markets', *Review of Economic Studies*, **80** (2), 429–62.

Bénabou, R. and J. Tirole (2016), 'Mindful Economics: The Production, Consumption, and Value of Beliefs', *Journal of Economic Perspectives*, **30** (3), 141–64.

Bennett, R.J. and G. Krebs (1994), 'Local Economic Development Partnerships: An Analysis of Policy Networks in EC-LEDA Local Employment Development Strategies', *Regional Studies*, **28**, 119–40.

Bentick, B.L. and M.K. Lewis (2004), 'Real Estate Speculation as a Source of Banking and Currency Instability: Some Different Lessons from the Asian Crisis', *Economics and Labour Relations Review*, **14** (2), 256–75.

Blanc-Brude, F., H. Goldsmith and T. Valila (2006), 'Ex-Ante Construction Costs in the European Road Sector: A Comparison of Public-Private Partnerships and Traditional Public Procurement', *EIB Economic and Financial Report 2006/01*, European Investment Bank.

Boardman, A. and M. Hellowell (2016), 'A Comparative Analysis and Evaluation of Specialist PPP Units' Methodologies for Conducting Value for Money Appraisals', *Journal of Comparative Policy Analysis: Research and Practice*, published online June 16, http://www.tandfonline.com/doi/abs/10.1080/13876988. 2016.1190083 JournalCode=fcpa20, accessed 18 June 2016.

Booth, M. and S. Hutchinson (2016), 'How Royal Adelaide Hospital's Cost Blew Out', *The Australian*, 6 April, 8.

Broadbent, J. and R. Laughlin (2003), 'Public Private Partnerships: An Introduction', *Accounting, Auditing and Accountability Journal*, **16** (3), 332–41.

Brown, C. (2005), 'Financing Transport Infrastructure: For Whom the Road Tolls', *Australian Economic Review*, **38** (4), 431–8.

Buchanan, James M. (1958), *Public Principles of Public Debt*, Homewood, IL: Richard D. Irwin.

Buchanan, James M. (1992), 'Public Debt', in P. Newman, M. Milgate and J. Eatwell (eds), *New Palgrave Dictionary of Money and Finance*, Vol. 3, London: Macmillan.

Buehler, R., D. Griffin and M. Ross (1994), 'Exploring the Planning Fallacy: Why People Underestimate Their Task Completion Times', *Journal of Personality and Social Psychology*, **67**, 366–81.

Buse, K. and G. Walt (2000a), 'Global Public–Private Partnerships: Part I – A New Development in Health?', *Bulletin of the World Health Organization*, **78** (4), 549–61.

Buse, K. and G. Walt (2000b), 'Global Public–Private Partnerships: Part II – What Are the Health Issues for Global Governance?', *Bulletin of the World Health Organization*, **78** (5), 699–709.

Buse, K. and A. Waxman (2001), 'Public–Private Health Partnerships: A Strategy for WHO', *Bulletin of the World Health Organization*, **79** (8), 748–54.

Campbell, D.J. (1988), 'Task Complexity: A Review and Analysis', *Academy of Management Review*, **13** (1), 40–52.

Cantarelli, C.C., B. Flyvbjerg and S.L. Buhl (2012), 'Geographical Variation in Project Cost Performance: The Netherlands versus Worldwide', *Journal of Transport Geography*, **24**, 324–431.

Cantarelli, C.C., B. Flyvbjerg, B. van Wee and E.J.E. Molin (2010), 'Lock-In and Its Influence on the Project Performance of Large-Scale Transportation Infrastructure Projects: Investigating the Way in Which Lock-In Can Emerge and Affect Cost Overruns', *Environment and Planning B: Planning and Design*, **73** (5), 792–807.

Carr, Bob (2020), 'Idiot Genius's Forces Will Continue with Their Wrecking', *The Weekend Australian*, 7–8 November, 11.

Casson, M. (2000), *Economics of International Business: A New Research Agenda*, Cheltenham, UK and Northampton, MA, USA: Edward Elgar Publishing.

Chandler, A.D. Jr (1990), *Scale and Scope: The Dynamics of Industrial Capitalism*, Cambridge, MA: Harvard University Press.

Clark, R.M. and S. Hakim (eds) (2019), *Public Private Partnerships: Construction, Protection, and Rehabilitation of Critical Infrastructure*, Cham, Switzerland: Springer.

Clarke, H. and A. Hawkins (2006), 'Economic Framework for Melbourne Traffic Planning', *Agenda*, **13** (1), 63–80.

Cox, J. (2005), 'Caught on the Road to Nowhere', *The Australian*, 28 November, 8.

Crouch, Brad (2020), 'RAH Shines in Pandemic', *The Advertiser*, 4 July, 10.

Cyert, R.M. and J.G. March (1963), *A Behavioural Theory of the Firm*, Englewood Cliffs, NJ: Prentice-Hall.

Daniels, R.J. and M.J. Trebilcock (1996), 'Private Provision of Public Infrastructure: An Organizational Analysis of the Next Privatization Frontier', *University of Toronto Law Journal*, **46**, 375–425.

De Clerck, Dennis (2015), 'Public-Private Partnership Procurement Game-Theoretic Studies of the Tender Process', Dissertation presented to obtain the degree of Doctor in Business Economics, KU Leuven, Faculty of Economics and Business, No. 490.

Engel, E., R.D. Fischer and A. Galetovic (2014), *The Economics of Public-Private Partnerships: A Basic Guide*, Cambridge: Cambridge University Press.

Epley, N. and T. Gilovich (2016), 'The Mechanics of Motivated Reasoning', *Journal of Economic Perspectives*, **30** (3), 133–40.

Ergas, Henry (2014), 'Wrong Way, Go Back: Mega Project Funding Muddle', *The Australian*, 13 January, 10.

Ernst & Young (EY) (2020), *Where to Now for the PPP Model?*, http://www.ey.com/en_au/strategy-transactions/where-to-now-for-the-ppp-model, accessed 5 November 2020.

Eurodad (2018), *History RePPPeated – How Public Private Partnerships Are Failing*, European Network on Debt and Development, http://eurodad.org/HistoryRePPPeated, accessed 3 March 2019.

European Court of Auditors (ECA) (2018), *Public Private Partnerships in the EU: Widespread Shortcomings and Limited Benefits*, Special Report 09/2018, https://www.eca.europa.eu/Lists/ECADocuments/SR18_09/SR_PPP_EN.pdf, accessed 15 August 2020.

European PPP Expertise Centre (EPEC) (2011), *The Non-Financial Benefits of PPPs: A Review of Concepts and Methodology*, https://www.eib.org/attachments/epec/epec_non_financial_benefits_of_ppps_en.pdf, accessed 3 March 2020.

European PPP Expertise Centre (EPEC) (2015), *PPP Motivations and Challenges for the Public Sector: Why (Not) and How*, https://www.eib.org/attachments/epec/epec_ppp_motivations_and_challenges_en.pdf, accessed 3 March 2020.

Festinger, Leon (1950), 'Informal Social Communication', *Psychological Review*, **57** (5), 271–82.

Festinger, Leon (1957), *A Theory of Cognitive Dissonance*, Stanford, CA: Stanford University Press.

Flyvbjerg, Bent (1996), 'The Dark Side of Planning: Rationality and *Realrationalität*', in S. Mandelbaum, L. Mazza and R. Burchell (eds), *Explorations in Planning Theory*, New Brunswick, NJ: Center for Urban Policy Research Press, 383–94.

Flyvbjerg, Bent (1998), *Rationality and Power: Democracy in Practice*, Chicago: University of Chicago Press.

Flyvbjerg, Bent (2003), 'Delusions of Success: Commentary on Dan Lovallo and Daniel Kahneman', *Harvard Business Review*, December, 121–3.

Flyvbjerg, Bent (2005), 'Machiavellian Megaprojects', *Antipode*, **37** (1), 18–22.

Flyvbjerg, Bent (2006), 'From Nobel Prize to Project Management: Getting Risks Right', *Project Management Journal*, **37**, 5–15.

Flyvbjerg, Bent (2008), 'Public Planning of Mega-Projects: Overestimation of Demand and Underestimation of Costs', in H. Priemus, B. Flyvbjerg and B. van Wee (eds), *Decision-Making on Mega-Projects: Cost–Benefit Analysis, Planning, and Innovation*, Cheltenham, UK and Northampton, MA, USA: Edward Elgar Publishing, 120–44.

Flyvbjerg, Bent (2009), 'Survival of the Unfittest: Why the Worst Infrastructure Gets Built, and What We Can Do about It', *Oxford Review of Economic Policy*, **25** (3), 344–67.

Flyvbjerg, Bent (2012), 'Why Mass Media Matter to Planning Research: The Case of Megaprojects', *Journal of Planning Education and Research*, **32** (2), 169–81.

Flyvbjerg, Bent (ed.) (2014), *Megaproject Planning and Management: Essential Readings*, Elgar Research Review, Cheltenham, UK and Northampton, MA, USA: Edward Elgar Publishing.

Flyvbjerg, Bent (2016), 'The Fallacy of Beneficial Ignorance: A Test of Hirschman's Hiding Hand', *World Development*, **84**, 176–89.

Flyvbjerg, B., N. Bruzelius and W. Rothengatter (2003), *Megaprojects and Risk: An Anatomy of Ambition*, Cambridge: Cambridge University Press.

Flyvbjerg, B., M.S. Holm and S. Buhl (2002), 'Underestimating Costs in Public Works Projects: *Error or Lie?*', *Journal of the American Planning Association*, **68** (3), 279–95.

Flyvbjerg, B., M.S. Holm and S. Buhl (2005), 'How (In)accurate Are Demand Forecasts in Public Works Projects?', *Journal of the American Planning Association*, **71**, 131–46.

Fouracre, P.R., R.J. Allport and J.M. Thomson (1990), *The Performance and Impact of Rail Mass Transit in Developing Countries*, TRRL Research Report 278, Crowthorne, UK: Transport and Road Research Laboratory.

Freeman, R.E. (1984), *Strategic Management: A Stakeholder Approach*, Boston, MA: Pitman.

Frick, Karen T. (2008), 'The Cost of the Technological Sublime: Daring Ingenuity and the New San Francisco–Oakland Bay Bridge', in H. Priemus, B. Flyvbjerg and B. van Wee (eds), *Decision-Making on Mega-Projects: Cost–Benefit Analysis, Planning, and Innovation*, Cheltenham, UK and Northampton, MA, USA: Edward Elgar Publishing, 239–62.

Geddes, R. Richard and Joshua K. Goldman (2015), 'Institutional Economics and the Cost of Capital', Cornell Program in Infrastructure Policy Working Paper, Ithaca, NY, 26 May.

Gelber, Frank (2014), 'BOOT is on the Other Foot for Infrastructure', *The Australian*, 1 May, 26.

Gerrard, Michael B. (2001), 'Public Private Partnerships', *Finance and Development*, **38** (3), September, 48–51, reprinted in Grimsey and Lewis (2005a).

Gilovich, T. (1991), *How We Know What Isn't So: The Fallibility of Human Reason in Everyday Life*, New York: Free Press.

Gleeson, T.P., D. Grimsey and M.K. Lewis (2019), 'How Successful Has the PPP Model Been in Australia', in R.M. Clark and S. Hakim (eds), *Public Private Partnerships: Construction, Protection, and Rehabilitation of Critical Infrastructure*, Cham, Switzerland: Springer, 167–92.

Greenspan, Stephen (2009), *Annals of Gullibility: Why We Get Duped and How to Avoid It*, Westport, CT: Praeger Publishers.

Grimsey, D. and M.K. Lewis (2002), 'Evaluating the Risks of Public Private Partnerships for Infrastructure Projects', *International Journal of Project Management*, **20** (2), 107–18, reprinted in Grimsey and Lewis (2005a).

Grimsey, D. and M.K. Lewis (2004a), 'The Governance of Contractual Relationships in Public Private Partnerships', *Journal of Corporate Citizenship*, **15**, 91–109.

Grimsey, D. and M.K. Lewis (2004b), *Public Private Partnerships: The Worldwide Revolution in Infrastructure Provision and Project Finance*, Cheltenham, UK and Northampton, MA, USA: Edward Elgar Publishing.

Grimsey, D. and M.K. Lewis (eds) (2005a), *The Economics of Public Private Partnerships*, The International Library of Critical Writings in Economics, Cheltenham, UK and Northampton, MA, USA: Edward Elgar Publishing.

Grimsey, D. and M.K. Lewis (2005b), 'Are Public Private Partnerships Value for Money? Evaluating Alternative Approaches and Comparing Academic and Practitioner Views', *Accounting Forum*, **29** (4), 345–78.

Grimsey, D. and M.K. Lewis (2007), 'Public Private Partnerships and Public Procurement', *Agenda: A Journal of Policy Analysis and Reform*, **14** (2), 171–88.

Grimsey, D. and M.K. Lewis (2009), 'Developing a Framework for Procurement Options Analysis', in A. Akintoye and M. Beck (eds), *Policy, Finance and Management for Public-Private Partnerships*, Oxford: Wiley-Blackwell, 398–413.

Grimsey, D. and M.K. Lewis (2011), 'Minimizing Collateral Damage: Options for Financing Public Private Partnerships in the Wake of the Financial Crisis', in Chris Green, Max Hall, Eric Pentecost and Tom Weyman-Jones (eds), *Financial Institutions, Systems and Markets*, Cheltenham, UK and Northampton, MA, USA: Edward Elgar Publishing, 249–65.

Grimsey, D. and M.K. Lewis (2017), *Global Developments in Public Infrastructure Procurement: Evaluating Public Private Partnerships and Other Procurement Options*, Cheltenham, UK and Northampton, MA, USA: Edward Elgar Publishing.

Grossman, S. and O. Hart (1986), 'The Costs and Benefits of Ownership: A Theory of Vertical and Lateral Integration', *Journal of Political Economy*, **94** (4), 691–719.

Grout, P. (1997), 'The Economics of the Private Finance Initiative', *Oxford Review of Economic Policy*, **13** (4), 53–66, reprinted in Grimsey and Lewis (2005a).

Grout, P.A. (2003), 'Public and Private Sector Discount Rates in Public-Private Partnerships', *Economic Journal*, **113** (486), C62–C68, reprinted in Grimsey and Lewis (2005a).

Grout, P.A. (2005), 'Value-for-Money Measurement in Public-Private Partnerships', *EIB Papers*, **10** (2), 33–56.

Harding, A. (1998), 'Public-Private Partnerships in the UK', in J. Pierre (ed.), *Partnerships in Urban Governance: European and American Experience*, New York: St. Martin's Press.

Harris, A. (1998), 'Credulity and Credibility in Infrastructure Funding', ACT Department of Urban Services Summer Seminar Series, Financing Urban Infrastructure and Services, University of Canberra, 6 March, www.audit.nsw.gov/au/publicvations/speeches/ag_speech/1998/uc6398.htm, accessed 30 April 2004.

Harris, A. (2006), 'Edited Transcript of *Four Corners* Interview', www.abc.net.au/4corners/content/2006/s1573798.htm, accessed 27 April 2007.

Hart, O. (2003), 'Incomplete Contracts and Public Ownership: Remarks, and an Application to Public-Private Partnerships', *Economic Journal*, **113** (486), C69–C76, reprinted in Grimsey and Lewis (2005a).

Hart, O. and J. Moore (1990), 'Property Rights and the Theory of the Firm', *Journal of Political Economy*, **98**, 1119–58.

Hicks, John (1983), *Classics and Moderns: Collected Essays on Economic Theory*, Vol. III, Oxford: Basil Blackwell.

Hirschman, A.O. (1967), 'The Principle of the Hiding Hand', *Public Interest*, **6**, 10–23.

HM Treasury (2003), *The Green Book: Appraisal and Evaluation in Central Government*, London: TSO.

Hodge, G.A. and C. Greve (2005), *The Challenge of Public-Private Partnerships: Learning from International Experience*, Cheltenham, UK and Northampton, MA, USA: Edward Elgar Publishing.

Hodge, G.A. and C. Greve (2017), 'On Public-Private Partnership Performance: A Contemporary Review', *Public Works Management and Policy*, **22** (1), 55–78.

Hodge, G.A. and C. Greve (2019), *The Logic of Public-Private Partnerships: The Enduring Interdependency of Politics and Markets*, Cheltenham, UK and Northampton, MA, USA: Edward Elgar Publishing.

Hodgson, G. (1995), 'Design and Build – Effects of Contractor Design on Highway Schemes', *Proceedings of the Institution of Civil Engineers – Civil Engineering*, **108** (2), 64–76, reprinted in Grimsey and Lewis (2005a).

Holland, R.C. (1984), 'The New Era in Public-Private Partnerships', in P.R. Porter and D.C. Sweet (eds), *Rebuilding America's Cities: Roads to Recovery*, New Brunswick, NJ: Center for Urban Policy Research.

Hood, Christopher (1995), 'The "New Public Management" in the 1980s: Variations on a Theme', *Accounting, Organizations and Society*, **20** (2/3), 93–100, reprinted in Grimsey and Lewis (2005a).

House of Commons Committee of Public Accounts (2006), *The Refinancing of the Norfolk and Norwich Hospital*, Thirty-fifth report of session 2005–06, May.

House of Commons Transport Committee (2008), *Select Committee on Transport Second Report*, 16 January, https://publications.parliament.uk/pa/cm200708/cmselect/cmtran/45/4509.htm, accessed 14 May 2021.

InfraDeals (2016), 'Inframation Deals', https://www.inframationnews.com/deals, accessed 16 April 2018.

Infrastructure Partnerships Australia (IPA) (2020), *Measuring the Value and Service Outcomes of Social Infrastructure PPPs in Australia and New Zealand*, https://www.researchgate.net/publication/340449377_Measuring_the_value_and_ service_outcomes_of_Social_Infrastructure_PPPs_in_Australia_and_New_Zealand, accessed 3 July 2020.

Irvine, Jessica (2013), 'Sydney Opera House Stands Tall as World's Worst Example of Mega-Project Planning', *The Advertiser*, 23 October, 20.

Janis, I.L. (1980), *Groupthink: Psychological Studies of Policy Decisions and Fiascos*, 2nd edn, New York: Houghton Mifflin.

Kahneman, D. (1994), 'New Challenges to the Rationality Assumption', *Journal of Institutional and Theoretical Economics*, **150**, 18–36.

Kahneman, D. (2011), *Thinking Fast and Slow*, New York: Farrar, Strauss, Giroux.

Kahneman, D. and A. Tversky (1979), 'Intuitive Prediction: Biases and Corrective Procedures', *Management Science*, **12**, 313–27.

Kay, J. (1993), 'Efficiency and Private Capital in the Provision of Infrastructure', in Organisation for Economic Co-operation and Development, *Infrastructure Policies for the 1990s*, Paris: OECD, 55–73.

Kenny, C. and M. Booth (2015), 'Adelaide Building Costs a World Beater', *The Australian*, 19 March, 1, 2.

Klein, M. (1997), 'The Risk Premium for Evaluating Public Projects', *Oxford Review of Economic Policy*, **13** (4), 29–42, reprinted in Grimsey and Lewis (2005a).

KPMG (2010), *Operating Healthcare Infrastructure: Analysing the Evidence*, https://www.ipfa.org/documents/operating-healthcare-infrastructureanalysing-the -evidence-kpmg/, accessed 30 March 2010.

Levitt, R.E. and K. Eriksson (2019), 'Mitigating PPP Governance Challenges: Lessons from Eastern Australia', in R.E. Levitt, W.R. Scott and M.J. Garvin (eds), *Public–Private Partnerships for Infrastructure Development: Finance, Stakeholder Alignment, Governance*, Cheltenham, UK and Northampton, MA, USA: Edward Elgar Publishing, 104–20.

Levitt, R.E., W.R. Scott and M.J. Garvin (eds) (2019), *Public–Private Partnerships for Infrastructure Development: Finance, Stakeholder Alignment, Governance*, Cheltenham, UK and Northampton, MA, USA: Edward Elgar Publishing.

Lewis, M.K. (1994), 'Banking on Real Estate', in D.E. Fair and R. Raymond (eds), *The Competitiveness of Financial Institutions and Centres in Europe*, Dordrecht: Kluwer.

Lewis, M.K. (2001), 'Finance, Private', in W.R. Prest (ed.), *Wakefield Companion to South Australian History*, Adelaide: Wakefield Press, 196–7.

Lewis, M.K. (2010), 'An Islamic Economic Perspective on the Global Financial Crisis', in Steve Kates (ed.), *Macroeconomic Economic Theory and Its Failings: Alternative Perspectives on the Global Financial Crisis*, Cheltenham, UK and Northampton, MA, USA: Edward Elgar Publishing, 159–83.

Lewis, M.K. (2011), 'Monetary Policies during the Financial Crisis: An Appraisal', in Steve Kates (ed.), *The Global Financial Crisis: What Have We Learnt?*, Cheltenham, UK and Northampton, MA, USA: Edward Elgar Publishing, 138–53.

Lewis, M.K. (2015), *Understanding Ponzi Schemes*, Cheltenham, UK and Northampton, MA, USA: Edward Elgar Publishing.

Lewis, M.K. and A. Kaleem (2019), *Religion and Finance: Comparing the Approaches of Judaism, Christianity and Islam*, Cheltenham, UK and Northampton, MA, USA: Edward Elgar Publishing.

Lind, R.C. (ed.) (1982), *Discounting for Time and Risk in Energy Policy*, Baltimore, MD: Johns Hopkins University Press.

Linder, S.H. (1999), 'Coming to Terms with the Public-Private Partnership: A Grammar of Multiple Meanings', *American Behavioral Scientist*, **43** (1), 35–51, reprinted in Grimsey and Lewis (2005a).

Linder, S.H. and P.V. Rosenau (2000), 'Mapping the Terrain of the Public-Private Policy Partnership', in P.V. Rosenau (ed.), *Public–Private Policy Partnerships*, Cambridge MA: MIT Press, 1–18.

Little, Richard (2011), 'The Emerging Role of Public-Private Partnerships in Megaproject Delivery', *Public Works Management and Policy*, **16** (3), 240–49.

Logan, J.R. and H.L. Molotch (1987), *Urban Fortunes: The Political Economy of Place*, Berkeley and Los Angeles, CA: University of California Press.

Lord, C., L. Ross and M. Lepper (1979), 'Biased Assimilation and Attitude Polarization: The Effects of Prior Theories on Subsequently Considered Evidence', *Journal of Personality and Social Psychology*, **37**, 2098–109.

Loussikian, Kylar (2016), 'Public-Private Road Deals Take Toll on Investors', *The Weekend Australian*, 4–5 June, 28.

Lovallo, D. and D. Kahneman (2003), 'Delusions of Success: How Optimism Undermines Executives' Decisions', *Harvard Business Review*, July, 56–63.

Mackie, P. and J. Preston (1998), 'Twenty-One Sources of Error and Bias in Transport Project Appraisal', *Transport Policy*, **5**, 1–7.

Macniel, I. (1974), 'The Many Futures of Contracts', *Southern California Law Review*, **47**, 691–816.

Makovšek, D. and D. Veryard (2016), 'The Regulatory Asset Base and Project Finance Models: An Analysis of Incentives for Efficiency', Discussion Paper 2016-01, International Transport Forum, Paris: OECD.

March, J.G. and H.A. Simon (1958), *Organizations*, New York: John Wiley and Sons.

Marglin, S.A. (1967), *Public Investment Criteria*, London: Allen and Unwin.

Marsilio, M., G. Cappellaro and C. Cuccurullo (2011), 'The Intellectual Structure of Research into PPPs', *Public Management Review*, **13** (6), 763–82.

Mascarenhas, Merruk (2009), 'The Quest for Community', Canadian Marketing Association, http://www.canadianmarketingblog.com/contributors/merril-mascarenhas/, accessed 7 September 2010.

McLaughlin, Kathleen and Stephen P. Osborne (2000), 'A One Way Street or Two-Way Traffic? Can Public-Private Partnerships Impact on the Policy-making Process?', in Stephen P. Osborne (ed.), *Public–Private Partnerships: Theory and Practice in International Perspective*, London and New York: Routledge, 324–38.

McQuaid, Ronald W. (2000), 'The Theory of Partnership: Why Have Partnerships?', in Stephen P. Osborne (ed.), *Public–Private Partnerships: Theory and Practice in International Perspective*, London and New York: Routledge, 9–35.

Miller, R. and X. Olleros (2000), 'Project Shaping as a Competitive Advantage', in R. Miller and D. Lessard (eds), *The Strategic Management of Large Engineering Projects: Shaping Institutions, Risks and Governance*, Cambridge, MA: MIT Press, 93–130.

Monk, A.H.B., R.E. Levitt, M.J. Garvin, A.J. South and G. Carollo (2019), 'Public–Private Partnerships for Infrastructure Delivery', in R.E. Levitt, W.R. Scott and M.J. Garvin (eds), *Public–Private Partnerships for Infrastructure Development: Finance, Stakeholder Alignment, Governance*, Cheltenham, UK and Northampton, MA, USA: Edward Elgar Publishing, 19–34.

Moszoro, Marian W. (2016), 'Public versus Private Cost of Capital with State-Contingent Terminal Value', https://papers.ssrn.com/sol3/papers.cfm?abid=2674668, accessed 20 April 2016.

Mott MacDonald (2002), *Review of Large Public Procurement in the UK*, London: HM Treasury.

National Centre for Social and Economic Modelling (2014), 'Welcome to the Welfare Nation: Half of Australia's Families Pay No Net Tax', news.com.au, 9 May, http://www.news.com.au/national/welcome-to-the-welfare-nation-half-of-australias-families-pay-no-net-tax/story-fncynjr2-1226911042149, accessed 23 June 2016.

National Research Council (NRC) (2005), *The Owner's Role in Project Risk Management*, Washington, DC: National Academies Press.

Nowacki, C. (2019), 'The Financier State: Infrastructure Planning and Asset Recycling in New South Wales, Australia', in R.E. Levitt, W.R. Scott and M.J. Garvin (eds), *Public–Private Partnerships for Infrastructure Development: Finance, Stakeholder Alignment, Governance*, Cheltenham, UK and Northampton, MA, USA: Edward Elgar Publishing, 246–64.

Officer, R.R. (2003), 'The Respective Roles of Government and the Private Sector and Private/Public Partnerships', *Public Private Partnerships Forum*, The Accounting Foundation, The University of Sydney, 8 December.

Osborne, D. and T. Gaebler (1993), *Reinventing Government: How the Entrepreneurial Spirit is Transforming the Public Sector*, New York: Penguin.

Osborne, Stephen (2000), *Public-Private Partnerships: Theory and Practice in International Perspective*, London: Routledge.

Pickrell, D.H. (1990), *Urban Rail Transit Projects: Forecast versus Actual Ridership and Cost*, Washington, DC: US Department of Transportation.

Porter, M. (1990), *The Comparative Advantage of Nations*, New York: Free Press.

PricewaterhouseCoopers France (PWC) (2011), *Étude sur la performance des contrats de partenariat*, Paris: Pricewaterhouse Coopers.

PricewaterhouseCoopers (PWC) (2017), *Reimagining Public Private Partnerships*, https://www.pwc.com.au/legal/assets/reimagining-ppps-oct17.pdf, accessed 3 December 2017.

Priemus, H., B. Flyvbjerg and B. van Wee (eds) (2008), *Decision-Making on Mega-Projects: Cost–Benefit Analysis, Planning, and Innovation*, Cheltenham, UK and Northampton, MA, USA: Edward Elgar Publishing.

Rebel report (2015), *Rebel Report on Risk, Discount Rates and Non-Valued Effects in VfM Assessment*, Annex to European PPP Expertise Centre (EPEC) (2011), *The Non-Financial Benefits of PPPs: A Review of Concepts and Methodology*, https://www.eib.org/attachments/epec/epec_non_financial_benefits_of_ppps_en .pdf, accessed 3 March 2020.

Rosenau, P.V. (2000), *Public-Private Policy Partnerships*, Cambridge, MA: The MIT Press.

Samuelson, Paul (1964), 'Principals of Efficiency: Discussion', *American Economic Review*, **81**, 191–209.

Sappington, D.E.M. (1991), 'Incentives in Principal-Agent Relationships', *Journal of Economic Perspectives*, **5**, 45–66.

Savas, E.S. (1982), *Privatizing the Public Sector: How to Shrink Government*, Chatham, NJ: Chatham House Publishers.

Savas, E.S. (1987), *Privatization: The Key to Better Government*, Chatham, NJ: Chatham House Publishers.

Savas, E.S. (2000), *Privatization and Public-Private Partnerships*, New York: Chatham House Publishers.

Sawyer, J.E. (1952), 'Entrepreneurial Error and Economic Growth', *Explorations in Entrepreneurial History*, **4** (4), 199–204.

Scott, W.R., R.E. Levitt and M.J. Garvin (2019), 'Introduction: PPPs – Theoretical Challenges and Directions Forward', in R.E. Levitt, W.R. Scott and M.J. Garvin (eds), *Public–Private Partnerships for Infrastructure Development: Finance, Stakeholder Alignment, Governance*, Cheltenham, UK and Northampton, MA, USA: Edward Elgar Publishing, 1–14.

Seldon, A. (1990), *Capitalism*, Oxford: Basil Blackwell

Sellgren, J. (1990), 'Local Economic Development Partnerships – An Assessment of Local Authority Economic Development Initiatives', *Local Government Studies*, **16** (4), July/August, 57–78.

Smith, R. and K. Narioka (2016), 'Toshiba Faces Power Meltdown', *Wall Street Journal*, reprinted in *The Australian*, 30 December, 16.

Solow, R.M. (1965), *Capital Theory and the Rate of Return*, Chicago: Rand McNally.

Survey of American Homeowners (2002), '2002 Coast vs. Value Report', *Remodeling*, 20 November.

Taleb, N.N. (2010), *The Black Swan: The Impact of the Highly Improbable*, 2nd edn, London: Penguin.

Thaler, R.H. (2016), 'Behavioral Economics: Past, Present, and Future', *American Economic Review*, **107** (7), July, 1577–600.

The Australian (2019), 'Brand Interviewed by Jeremy Paxman on the BBC', 25 October 2013, quoted in *Cut & Paste*, 4 March, 13.

The Economist (2017), 'Fat Tails', *The Economist*, 7–13 January, 23–4.

The Economist (2019a), 'Millenial socialism', *The Economist*, 16 February, 9.

The Economist (2019b), 'Life, Liberty and the Pursuit of Property', *The Economist*, 16 February, 16–20.

The Guardian (2018a), 'Bye-Bye, PFI: UK Signals Effective End of Private Finance Initiative', https://www.globalconstructionreview.com/sectors/bye-bye-pfi-uk-sig nals-effective-end-private-finan/, accessed 9 July 2020.

The Guardian (2018b), 'Hammond Abolishes PFI Contracts for New Infrastructure Projects', https://www.theguardian.com/uk-news/2018/oct/29/hammond-abolishes-pfi-contracts-for-new-infrastructure-projects, accessed 29 October 2018.

The Scottish Office (1993), *Progress in Partnership: A Consultation Paper on the Future of Urban Regeneration Policy in Scotland*, Edinburgh: HMSO.

The Sentencing Project (2019), 'Private Prisons in the United States', https://www.sentencingproject.org/publications/private-prisons-united-states/, accessed 15 August 2020.

Thornton, E. (2007), 'Roads to Riches', *Business Week*, 7 May, 50–57.

Trujillo, A., R. Cohen, X. Freixas and R. Sheehy (1998), 'Infrastructure Financing with Unbundled Mechanisms', *The Financier*, **5** (4), 10–27, reprinted in Grimsey and Lewis (2005a).

Turvey, R. (ed.) (1968), *Public Enterprise*, Penguin Modern Economics, Harmondsworth, UK: Penguin.

Uplekar, M., S. Juvekar, S. Morankar, S. Rangan and P. Nunn (1998), 'Tuberculosis Patients and Practitioners in Private Clinics in India', *International Journal of Tuberculosis and Lung Disease*, **2** (4), 324–9.

Uplekar, M., V. Pathania and M. Raviglione (2001), 'Private Practitioners and Public Health: Weak Links in Tuberculosis Control', *Lancet*, **358** (9285), 912–16.

UK House of Commons Committee of Public Accounts (2011), *Lessons from PFI and Other Projects (Public Accounts Committee, Forty-Fourth Report)*, oral evidence given by senior public officials, London: UK House of Commons, The Stationery Office, https://publications.parliament.uk/pa/cm201012/cmselect/cmpubacc/1201/1201.pdf, accessed 3 May 2020.

Vickrey, W. (1964), 'Principals of Efficiency: Discussion', *American Economic Review*, **54**, 88–92.

Vives, Antonio, Juan Benavides and Angela M. Paris (2010), 'Selecting Infrastructure Delivery Modalities: No Time for Ideology or Semantics', *Journal of Construction Engineering and Management*, **136** (4), April, 412–18.

Wachs, M. (1989), 'When Planners Lie with Numbers', *Journal of the American Planning Association*, **55** (4), 476–9.

Weinstein, N.D. (1980), 'Unrealistic Optimism about Future Life Events', *Journal of Personality and Social Psychology*, **39**, 806–20.

Wikipedia (2019), 'Megaproject', https://en.wikipedia.org/wiki/Megaproject, accessed 11 March 2019.

Williamson, O.E. (1985), *The Economic Institution of Capitalism: Firms, Markets, Relational Contracting*, New York: The Free Press.

Williamson, O.E. (1996), *The Mechanisms of Governance*, Oxford: Oxford University Press.

World Bank (1994), *World Development Report 1994: Infrastructure for Development*, New York: Oxford University Press.

Wright, S., J. Barlow and J.J. Roehrich (2019), 'Public-Private Partnerships for Health Services: Construction, Protection and Rehabilitation of Critical Healthcare Infrastructure in Europe', in R.M. Clark and S. Hakin (eds), *Public Private Partnerships: Construction, Protection, and Rehabilitation of Critical Infrastructure*, Cham, Switzerland: Springer, 125–51.

Zerunyan, F.V. (2019), 'Well-Designed Public Private Partnerships', in R.M. Clark and S. Hakin (eds), *Public Private Partnerships: Construction, Protection, and Rehabilitation of Critical Infrastructure*, Cham, Switzerland: Springer, 17–35.

Zweig, Jason (2009), 'How to Ignore the Yes-Man in Your Head', *Wall Street Journal*, 19 November, https://www.wsj.com/articles/SB10001424052748703811604574533680037778184, reprinted in *Wealth, The Australian*, 25 November 2009, 12.

Index

Seldon, A. 65
Sellgren, J. 25
service providers 108–9
serviced infrastructure model 111, 116
services
    focus on 40
    to include in the bundle 82
shadow tolls 54
sharing of responsibility 29, 41
Simon, H.A. 55
Smetters, K. 62
Smith, A. 65
social infrastructure 32–3, 44, 107–9
soft infrastructure 32–3
Spain 11–13
special purpose vehicle (SPV) 40, 56,
    110, 111–12
stakeholders 57, 79–80
standard PPP contracts 52
suitability of PPPs for infrastructure
    applications 122–3
sunk-cost fallacy 92
Sunshine Coast University Hospital 100
Sweden 6–8
'swinging pendulum' 17–19, 24
Sydney Opera House 97–8

Taleb, N.N. 89
Tata Mundra Ultra Mega Power project 7
taxation risk 61–4
taxes 47
    income tax 51–2
technical uncertainty 55–6
Thatcher, M. 22
The Economist 24
The Guardian 5, 6, 59, 64, 74
Tirole, J. 94
toll bridges 17, 48
toll roads 17, 48, 51, 54, 80
traditional public sector procurement
    34–5, 36
    reassessing 37–9
Trans-European Transport Network
    (TEN) motorway network 15
Trebilcock, M.J. 45
Trujillo, A. 44
Trump, D. 106
Tullock, G. 21
tunnelling 84, 115

Tversky, A. 91

unbundling 43–5, 66
uncertainty 56, 89, 105, 122
    technical 55–6
    see also risk
United Kingdom (UK) 52
    Fazakerley prison 52–3
    hospitals 119–20
    National Audit Office (NAO) 38–9,
        99, 119
    National Health Service (NHS)
        119
    ownership rights 43
    Private Finance Initiative (PFI) 5–6,
        38–9, 59, 64, 71, 74, 99, 118
    privatization 22
    Treasury 5–6, 59, 117
    see also House of Commons
United States of America (US) 32, 48,
    54, 91
    private prisons 2–3
    privatism 66
    privatization 22–3
    San Francisco Transbay Terminal 97
    tax-exempt bonds 47
user-pay PPPs 53–4, 80; *see also* toll
    bridges; toll roads

value for money (VfM) 67–9, 108, 119,
    121
    test 65, 69
Veryard, D. 119–20
Victorian Comprehensive Cancer Centre
    (VCCC) 100
Vives, A. 18–19

Wachs, M. 96
Weinstein, N.D. 93
'white elephants' 51, 104
whole-of-life-cycle costing 40–41, 76–7,
    120
wider social benefits 69, 72–3
Williamson, O. 20
World Bank 8, 20, 37–8
World Health Organization 20
Wright, S. 82

Zerunyan, F.V. 75